INSIDE of a DOG

WHAT DOGS SEE, SMELL, AND KNOW

ALEXANDRA HOROWITZ

Young Readers Edition

Simon & Schuster Books for Young Readers

New York London Toronto Sydney New Delhi

SIMON & SCHUSTER BOOKS FOR YOUNG READERS
An imprint of Simon & Schuster Children's Publishing Division
1230 Avenue of the Americas, New York, New York 10020

SIMON & SCHUSTER BOOKS FOR YOUNG READERS is a trademark of Simon & Schuster, Inc.
For information about special discounts for bulk purchases, please contact Simon & Schuster
Special Sales at 1-866-506-1949 or business@simonandschuster.com.
The Simon & Schuster Speakers Bureau can bring authors to your live event.
For more information or to book an event, contact the Simon & Schuster Speakers Bureau
at 1-866-248-3049 or visit our website at www.simonspeakers.com.
Book design by Lucy Ruth Cummins
The text for this book is set in Adobe Caslon Pro.
The illustrations for this book are rendered in pen and ink.
Manufactured in the United States of America
0216 FFG
2 4 6 8 10 9 7 5 3 1
CIP data for this book is available from the Library of Congress.
ISBN 978-1-4814-5093-5
ISBN 978-1-4814-5095-9 (eBook)

To Pumpernickel

CONTENTS

Preface

Like many of you picking up this book, I grew up with dogs. In my case these dogs were part of the family: They were allowed in the house, sometimes in our beds with us, and they were loved. But they were also a little different than the other members of the family. With our dogs, we trained them, took them for walks, and in between, we spent a lot of time ignoring them. They were always *there*, in the house, but they weren't always there, on our mind. When we went swimming, or to school, or to play with friends, my parents put the dogs outside in a yard or fenced area, or even (these were slightly different times—this wouldn't be considered responsible today) let them run loose in the neighborhood.

Years later, as a young adult living on my own, I adopted my own dog, Pumpernickel. I lived in a small apartment near a college: I didn't have a yard or fenced area. So I became more aware of how long I left her alone waiting for me to come back—largely because I was the one who took her out to pee, and I was the one who received her relieved greeting when I'd return to a dark apartment at night. Over the years, moving through many states, schools, and jobs, Pump stayed with me. She was my constant companion. I started racing home after work and school to be with her. I would bring her with me when I could. I hired dog walkers to keep her company when I was gone for a long time. I saw how much she brought to my life, and worried about giving her a good life in return.

But it took becoming a scientist of animal behavior to *really* change the way I saw her and dealt with her. When I began studying dogs, looking carefully at what they did when interacting with other dogs, with people, and how they behaved when on their own, I started to see my Pump in a whole new light. I was amazed. This book is all about what I discovered. From my own research and others studying dog behavior and cognition (what dogs do and what they know), I learned things about the mind of the dog that have entirely changed how I dealt with Pump and the dogs I have known since.

I write a lot about the joy of just *being* with dogs, though this book is mostly about the *science* of dogs. That might be intimidating to some people, but I suspect that since you picked up and are reading this book, it's not intimidating to you. Science is a powerful approach to looking at the world: By observing things and testing our hypotheses, we find out much more than when we simply make assumptions. And you, young reader, are in the perfect position to see the dog scientifically.

I wish I had had this book, or something like it, when I was your age. Not because this book has all the answers about dogs—it doesn't (and here's a secret: no book does!)—but because this book is all about a way of thinking about dogs that makes sense to me. It's a way to think about and treat the dogs you meet, live with, and love, that doesn't ignore them. Instead, it takes the slightly radical stance of putting the dog in the center of the picture, and taking the dog's point of view. That point of view is *terrifically neat*, and, if I may say so, a bit mind-blowing.

There is a lot more scientific work to be done in understanding what dogs see, smell, and know. Maybe *you* will do it! Science that helps you think about what it might be like to be a dog—or any animal—will go a long way toward giving dogs their due.

Now, go snuggle up near a dog you love and start reading. If your dog lays his head across the book, I don't mind. Read *your dog* instead. That's what I did, and boy, I'm glad I did.

Introduction

First, you see the head. Over the crest of the hill appears a muzzle, drooling. Long, jangly limbs come next, supporting a body that weighs at least 140 pounds. A wolfhound, three feet tall at his shoulder and five feet long from snout to tail, spies a long-haired Chihuahua hidden in the grass. The Chihuahua is six pounds, each of them trembling.

With one leap, the wolfhound lands in front of the Chihuahua. The Chihuahua looks away. The wolfhound bends down and nips at the Chihuahua's side. The Chihuahua looks back at the hound, who raises his rear end, tail held high, prepared to attack. Instead of fleeing, the Chihuahua matches the pose. She leaps onto the wolfhound's face, gripping his nose with her tiny paws. They begin to play.

For five minutes these dogs tumble, grab, bite, and lunge at each other. The wolfhound throws himself onto his side. The little dog attacks face, belly, and paws. A swipe by the hound sends the Chihuahua scurrying back. The hound barks, jumps up, and lands on his feet with a thud. The Chihuahua races toward one of those feet and bites it, hard. The hound has his mouth entirely around the Chihuahua, the little dog kicking at his big face, when the wolfhound's owner snaps a leash onto the hound's collar and pulls him away. The Chihuahua gets up, looks after them, barks as if to call them back, and then trots over to her owner.

These dogs hardly look as if they could be from the same species. How can they play so easily together? The wolfhound bit and charged at the Chihuahua. He had her entire body in his mouth. Yet the little dog was not frightened. She treated the huge dog just as he treated her.

Why doesn't the hound see the Chihuahua as a meal? Why doesn't the Chihuahua see the wolfhound as a threat? There are two ways to find out.

One is to be born as a dog. The other is to spend a lot of time carefully observing dogs. I couldn't do the first one, so I had to do the second. Come along as I describe what I have learned by watching.

* * *

I am a dog person.

My home has always had a dog in it. My love for dogs began with Heidi, a springer spaniel. Then there was Aster, with his blue eyes, lopped tail, and nighttime neighborhood ramblings. Up late, in my pajamas, I'd wait for his return. Later, when I was a college student, a chow mix named Beckett watched patiently as I left for the day.

And now at my feet lies the warm, curly, panting form of Pumpernickel—*Pump*—a mutt who has lived with me for sixteen years. As anyone who is a dog person will understand, I cannot imagine my life without this dog.

I am a dog person, and I am also a scientist.

I study animal behavior. I have learned the science of careful observations, of gathering and analyzing information. I have also spent many hours in the local dog parks and beaches with Pumpernickel. After a while, I began to look at the dogs there as I looked at other animals I have studied.

Once I had simply watched and smiled as Pumpernickel played with the local bull terrier. Then I came to understand how difficult it is to do what these two dogs were doing. They were doing a complex dance that required cooperation, split-second communication, and the ability to understand what the other dog wanted. The slightest turn of a head or the point of a nose seemed full of meaning.

I began bringing a video camera along and taping our outings at the park. At home I watched the tapes of dogs playing with each other, of people tossing balls and Frisbees for their pets. I watched tapes of chasing, fighting, petting, running, barking.

What I saw in these movies were snapshots of the minds of dogs. Dogs communicated with each other. Dogs tried to communicate with their owners. Dogs watched other dogs and people, figuring out what their actions meant. All of this gave me glimpses of the way the dogs were thinking.

I never saw Pumpernickel—or any dog—the same way again.

In this book I will introduce you to the science of the dog. We can begin to create a picture of the dog from the inside—of the skill of his nose, what he hears, how his eyes turn to us, and the brain behind it all.

This is not a dog-training book. Still, some of the information in it might lead you to be able to train your dog without even realizing it. This might catch us up with dogs, who (without reading any books) have already learned how to train people, often without the people even noticing.

Training is usually about changing a dog so that he can behave in ways a human will approve of. But my goal in this book is to look at what dogs actually are, not at what people want dogs to be. We are trying to understand what your dog wants from and understands about you.

I've gotten inside the dog and have glimpsed the dog's point of view. You can do the same. If you have a dog in the room with you, what you see in that great, furry pile of dogness is about to change.

A note on calling a dog "the dog": When scientists study animals, they are usually trying to figure out what is true about all of those animals, about the entire species. But of course scientists cannot put an entire species in a lab. So they study a few animals at a time. If they design their experiments well, what they find out about those few animals can tell us something about all similar animals.

So when I say something about "a dog" or "the dog" in this book, I am actually talking about "all the dogs who have been studied by scientists." Not all dogs are the same. Your dog may be different from the dogs who have been studied so far. Maybe your dog is an unusually good smeller, or never looks you in the eye, or loves his dog bed, or hates to be touched on his head. We can study dogs in general and write about dogs in general, but always, every dog is different.

In this book, I usually call a dog "him" unless I am writing about a dog I know to be a female. This is merely for convenience, and because "it" simply sounds wrong, as you know if you have ever known and loved a dog.

FROM THE DOG'S POINT OF NOSE

This morning I am woken up by Pump coming over to the bed and sniffing at me. Her nose is millimeters from my face, her whiskers grazing my lips. She suddenly sneezes explosively, an exclamation point on her greeting. I open my eyes and she is gazing at me, smiling, panting a hello.

Go look at a dog. Go on, look—maybe at one lying near you right now, curled around his folded legs on a dog bed, or sprawled on his side on the floor. Take a good look. And now forget everything you know about this or any other dog.

Okay, I admit it—you can't really forget all that you know. I don't expect you to forget your dog's name or his favorite food. But humor me and try. We are going to be looking at dogs through the lens of science, and science asks us to set aside what we think we already know and focus instead on what we can prove.

It will turn out that some of what we thought all along about our dogs is true, and other things that appear obvious are more doubtful than anyone knew. And when we try looking from a new point of view—from the point of view of dogs themselves—new ideas may arise in our minds. So the best way to begin understanding dogs is by forgetting what we think we already know.

The first thing to do is to stop thinking of your dog as if he is a human being.

It's easy to make this mistake. We think about our dogs as if they are people, because being people is something that we easily understand. *Of course*, we say, dogs love and long for things; of course they dream and think. We believe dogs know and understand us, feel bored, get jealous, and get depressed. We believe our dogs do all these things because *we* do all these things. But we'll come to a better understanding of dogs if we start with what *dogs*—not people—can actually feel, know, and understand.

We understand human experiences the best. So it's simplest for us to explain our dogs by imagining that their experiences are just like ours. If a person's eyes look mournful and she sighs loudly, we can figure out that she is sad, maybe even depressed. If your dog does the same thing, is it safe to say that he is sad? Depressed?

Sometimes we're right when we assume that dogs have feelings and reactions that match ours. Maybe our dogs really *are* depressed. Maybe sometimes they're also jealous, curious, or extremely interested in having a peanut butter sandwich for lunch. But maybe they're not.

If we see an animal's mouth turn up at the corners, we might think that the animal is happy. But a dolphin isn't happy just because its mouth turns up—its mouth is made that way. A chimpanzee who shows his teeth in a grin is actually making a sign of fear and submission. He's about as far from happy as a chimpanzee gets.

A human who raises her eyebrows is usually surprised. A capuchin monkey who does the same thing is not surprised—he's signaling to nearby monkeys that he is friendly. A baboon who raises his eyebrows, however, is making a deliberate threat. (So be careful when raising your eyebrows at a monkey.)

If we think only in terms of what humans want or do or like, we can end up missing or ignoring things animals do when they are simply being animals.

TAKE MY RAINCOAT, PLEASE

For instance, many dog owners have noticed that their dogs resist going outside when it's raining. From this observation, they come to a conclusion: My dog does not like rain.

So the owner buys the dog a raincoat.

My dog does not like rain. What does this mean? Does it mean that the dog dislikes getting rain on his body? It seems likely. Most humans, after all, do not like getting wet in the rain. But does that make the same thing true for dogs? We can look at the dog himself for evidence. The dog can't speak up to say how he feels about the rain, so we must look at what the dog does.

Is the dog excited and wagging when you get the raincoat out? This seems to suggest that the conclusion is true—the dog does not like rain and appreciates the raincoat because it keeps the rain off his fur. But there's another possible explanation for this behavior: Maybe the dog is simply excited because he knows the raincoat means that he is (finally!) going for a walk.

More evidence is needed. Does the dog flee from the raincoat? Curl his tail under his body and duck his head? This suggests that the conclusion is not true: The dog doesn't like the raincoat.

What about how the dog behaves when his fur is actually wet with rain? Does he look bedraggled? Does he shake the water off excitedly? What does this mean? It's hard to be sure. The dog's behavior is not giving us a clear answer here. Does he mind the rain or doesn't he? Does he need a raincoat or not?

We need some more clues, so we could take a look at some animals closely related to dogs—wolves. Both dogs and wolves, obviously, have their own coats on all the time. One coat is enough; when it rains, wolves may seek shelter, but they don't try to cover up with, say, leaves or branches. This suggests that dogs, too—except those with little or no fur—do not need an extra coat to protect them from the rain.

And a raincoat is something more than protection from falling water. A raincoat is a covering. It feels snug on your body. It presses on the back, chest, and sometimes the head of a dog who is wearing it. There *are* times when wolves get pressed upon the back or the head—when they are being scolded or "dominated" by another wolf.

A "dominant" animal is one who has authority over another, "submissive," animal. A dominant wolf is usually older, stronger, and larger than a submissive wolf. Sometimes, a wolf who is trying to show his dominance will pin another wolf by the snout, or actually stand over the other wolf. The wolf underneath will feel the pressure of the wolf's body on top of him. The pressure of a raincoat on a dog's back might feel similar.

For a person, wearing a raincoat feels like being protected from water in the air. For a dog, wearing a raincoat might feel like being told that another, stronger animal is nearby.

Is this the best interpretation of the dog's behavior? Looking at the evidence will tell us. Most dogs, when they are getting put into a raincoat, freeze in place. (You might see the same behavior when a dog who is getting a bath stops struggling when his fur gets heavy with water or a heavy towel is placed over him.) This is what a submissive wolf does—hold still to show he accepts the other animal's authority.

Ultimately, we can correctly conclude that a dog wearing a coat may go out peaceably into the rain, but it is not because he hates the rain or he likes the raincoat. It is because the coat makes him feel that someone else is in control.

If we think about what human beings are like—we don't like being wet and we want to protect our bodies from water—we'll come to the wrong conclusion about dogs and raincoats. If we look at what dogs (and their close relatives, wolves) actually *do*, then we'll come to a conclusion that is more likely to be true.

AN ANIMAL'S WORLD AND HIS *UMWELT*

In most cases, it is simple to start thinking of the dog as a dog and not as a small, furry human. All you have to do is to ask the dog what he wants. Then you must learn to translate his answer.

The first tool you'll need in getting that answer is this: understanding the point of view of the dog.

Each dog—each animal—has a point of view. Even more, each animal has its own world. It is a world made up of all the things the animals can see, smell, hear, or sense in some other way. It is a world made up of all the things that matter to the animal, that could help it or harm it, that are worth its notice or important for its life.

One scientist coined a word for it: *umwelt*, or "self-world." (You say it OOM-velt.) A creature's *umwelt* is made up of all the things that matter to that creature—all the things it notices or needs, can eat or sleep on or climb or fight with or run away from.

For example, consider the tick.

You probably haven't thought much about them. Maybe you've found one or two of these pests on your dog. It would be surprising if you had taken the time to consider what the world of a tick is like.

But take that time now.

Soon after hatching, a young tick climbs to a high perch—say, a blade of grass. Here's where things get interesting. Of all the sights, sounds, and smells in the world, the adult tick is waiting for just one. It is not looking around; ticks are blind. Sounds don't interest it. Only one thing will get a reaction from that tick: a whiff of butyric acid, a chemical given off by all warm-blooded creatures (like us—and dogs). We can sometimes smell it in sweat.

The tick might wait for that smell for a day, a month, or even up to a dozen years. Once it smells that precise odor, it drops off its perch. The tick's body is sensitive to warmth, and now it begins searching for a source of warmth and scurrying toward it. If the tick is lucky, it will reach the warm, sweaty being it has sensed nearby, climb aboard, and drink a meal of blood. After eating once, it drops off, lays eggs, and dies.

The point of all this is that the tick's world, its *umwelt*, is different from ours in astonishing ways. All that matters to the tick is smell and warmth, and so those two things are what it notices. The wind that whisks through the grass? Doesn't matter to the tick. The sounds of a child's birthday party? The tick doesn't care. The delicious crumbs of cake dropped on the ground? The tick doesn't notice that they are there.

The tick has four simple jobs—it mates, waits, drops, and feeds. So the tick's universe is divided into things that help it do these jobs, and things that do not matter. Its *umwelt* is made up of ticks and non-ticks, things it can climb on and things it cannot climb on, surfaces it might or might not drop onto, and things that it may or may not want to eat. Nothing else matters to the tick. Nothing else is part of its *umwelt*.

We humans have an *umwelt* too. In our *umwelt* we pay a lot of attention to where other people are and to what they are saying. (A tick, on the other hand, could not care less about a beautiful song or funny joke.) We see and hear the things that reach our eyes and ears, and we can smell strong odors that are right in front of our noses. There are other things going on all around us—the cry of a bat, too high-pitched for our ears to hear, or the smell of what a passerby had for dinner last night—but because they are not part of our *umwelt*, they mean nothing to us.

The same object might exist in several creatures' world, but it will mean different things to each. To a human being, a rose is a certain kind of flower, a romantic gift, or a thing of beauty. To a beetle, a rose might be an entire world, with places to hide, hunt, or lay eggs. To an elephant, a rose might be a thorn barely noticeable as it is crushed underfoot.

And to a dog? In a dog's *umwelt*, a rose is not a beautiful object or an entire world. A rose is just one part of all the plants that surround the dog. It is not particularly notable unless it has been urinated on by another dog, stepped on by another animal, or handled by the dog's owner. Then the rose becomes a thing of vivid interest, and it matters more to the dog than even the most beautiful rose might matter to us.

To understand a dog, we must do our best to enter his *umwelt*, to experience the world as a dog sees, hears, and (most importantly) smells it. Let's try it now.

Try smelling every object that you come across in the space of an afternoon.

Try listening to all the sounds around you now, the ones that you normally tune out. Can you hear a fan behind you, a beeping truck backing up in the street outside, the murmurs of far-off voices, someone nearby shifting in a chair, your own heart beating, a gulp as you swallow? If you could hear like a dog, you might notice these things plus a pen scratching on paper, the sound of a plant stretching as it grows, the cries of the insects that are always around us.

Drop down on the floor. Spending a bit of time at the height of your dog is surprising. What does the world look like down there? What do you notice? What becomes important to you?

Of course, even if you are down on your hands and knees, you are not seeing the objects in a room exactly as a dog sees them. A dog looking around a room does not think he is surrounded by human things; he sees *dog things*. Some dog things are the same as human things. Some are different.

A person sees a chair as a thing-to-be-sat-upon. A dog might see it that way too. The dog also sees the sofa, a pile of pillows, and the lap of a person on the floor as things-to-be-sat-upon. But he probably doesn't see a stool that way, although a person might. To a dog, a stool is more like an-obstacle-in-the-way.

A dog and a person are both likely to see a peanut butter sandwich as something-to-be-eaten. But to a dog, things-that-can-be-eaten is a wider category than it is to a person. Garbage isn't on a human list of menu items, but it is on a dog's.

Dogs have categories of their own—things-that-are-good-to-roll-in, for example. And dogs don't notice or care about many items that matter to humans—forks, knives, hammers, pushpins, fans, clocks, and so on. A dog cannot do anything to or with a clock, so the clock isn't part of the dog's *umwelt*. A dog cannot hammer a nail, so the dog doesn't care about the hammer—unless he notices the wooden handle and puts the hammer in the category of things-that-can-be-chewed.

ALEXANDRA HOROWITZ

A clash of *umwelts* can happen when a dog and a human see the same object in different ways. For instance, many dog owners insist that the dog is never to lie on the bed. Perhaps the owner will go out and purchase a large pillow, labeled a "dog bed." The dog will be encouraged to lie on this special bed, the non-forbidden bed. The dog will do so, sometimes reluctantly. And the dog owner feels successful: no dog on the bed!

Or is there? Many days I returned home to find a warm, rumpled pile of sheets on my bed and a wagging dog greeting me at the door.

The reason this happens becomes clear when we think about how a dog's world is different from a human's world. To a human, the difference between the dog bed and the human bed is obvious. The dog bed is low on the floor; the human bed is higher. The dog bed has a plain covering; the human bed has sheets and pillows. The dog bed is for dogs; the human bed is for humans. We would never be tempted to curl up on the dog bed. We expect the dog to feel the same way about the human bed.

What about the dog? Dogs don't generally see beds as special places for sleeping at all. They sleep and rest where they can, and prefer places that allow them to stretch out or curl up, where the temperature feels good, where there are other members of their family nearby, and where they feel safe. Any flattish surface in your home probably meets a dog's definition of a decent place to sleep.

So does a dog see the same clear difference between the dog bed and the human bed that we do? Probably not. Here's what your dog is likely to notice about your bed: It smells like you. It's a place where you relax, where you leave clothes, where you might drop crumbs. All those things make it a wonderful place to sleep. Better than the dog bed by far.

ASKING DOGS

Beginning to understand a dog's *umwelt* is the first step in understanding what's happening inside a dog. The next step is learning to understand the ways a dog talks to you.

It's easy to ask a dog a question—say, if he's happy or sad. There's no problem with the question. It makes perfect sense. The problem is that we have a very hard time understanding the answer.

Language makes us terribly lazy. If a friend of mine is

ALEXANDRA HOROWITZ

behaving strangely, I might spend weeks trying to figure out what's up with her—or I could take a shortcut and ask her. She'll tell me.

Dogs, on the other hand, never answer the way we'd hope. They don't reply to questions in well-punctuated sentences. Still, if we look, they have plainly answered.

> Licks are Pump's way of making contact, as though reaching out a hand. She greets me when I come home with licks to my face as I bend to pet her. I get waking licks to my hand as I nap in a chair. She licks my legs clean of salty sweat after a run. Sitting beside me, she pins my hand with her front leg and pushes open my fist to lick the soft warm flesh of my palm. I adore her licks.

When you arrive home from school, your dog may happily lick your face or your hand. "Kisses" are what a lot of dog owners call these licks: slobbery licks to the face, focused licking of a hand, or tongue-polishing an arm or leg.

When people kiss someone, it's because we love them. We assume that dogs do the same thing. Even the great scientist Charles Darwin was sure that licks mean affection. He wrote that dogs "have a striking way of exhibiting their affection: namely, by licking the hands or faces of their masters."

Was Darwin right? My dog's kisses feel affectionate

to me. But is the dog *trying to show* affection?

Dogs and wolves can answer this question for us, if we look at their behavior.

First, the bad news. Adult wolves, foxes, coyotes, and other wild dogs leave their puppies at their dens while they hunt. When a parent returns, the puppies eagerly lick the adult's face and muzzle. In response to the licks, the parent vomits some food and the pups gobble it up. The pups lick their parent's face to get fed.

Your dog must be so disappointed that, no matter how much he licks your face, you've never thrown up lunch for him to eat.

There's also another fact to consider—our mouths taste great to dogs. Dogs can taste most of the same things humans taste. They are enthusiastic about our food. Once I started thinking about it, it didn't take long for me to realize that Pumpernickel's licks to my face often happened just after a nice meal had gone into that face.

So if your dog licks your face, he could simply be excited because you taste like something delicious, and he'd love to share. This is how mouth licking started out: as a way for wolf pups to get their parents to give them some nicely pre-digested food. But it has also become something else.

Adult dogs and wolves lick muzzles simply to welcome another dog back home, and to get a report, by smelling, of where the newcomer has been or what he has done. Mothers clean their pups by licking, but they also give a few quick licks when they are back together after a time apart. A younger or timid dog may lick at the muzzle of a bigger dog to show he will not be aggressive or start a fight. Dogs who are familiar with each other may lick when they meet in the street. Perhaps this lick, along with a nice sniff, helps them be sure that the dog bounding toward them is who they think it is.

What began as a way for puppies to get a meal became a way for dogs and wolves to greet each other. These greeting licks often go along with wagging tails, mouths opened playfully, and general excitement. All of this behavior of dogs with other dogs shows us something about what your dog's behavior means with you. A dog doesn't kiss you for the same reason another human being might kiss you—but when a dog licks your face, it is indeed a way to say that he is glad you've finally come home.

To answer these kinds of questions about dogs, we have to understand a dog's world, its *umwelt*. The next chapters will help us do that. First, we will look at how dogs came from wolves, and the changes that happened to them along the way. Then, we must understand how a dog's senses work. We need to appreciate what a dog smells, sees, and hears, and imagine the view from two feet off the ground. Finally, we'll take a look at how the brain of a dog works.

Together, all of these pieces will combine to start to give us an answer to these questions: How does a dog think? What can a dog know? What does a dog understand?

BELONGING TO THE HOUSE

She's waiting just outside the kitchen, just beyond underfoot. Somehow Pump knows exactly where "out of the kitchen" is. Here she sprawls, and when I bring food to the table, she ducks into the kitchen to retrieve the fallen bits. At the table, she gets a little of everything, and she gives everything a try, although she may just roll it around in her mouth before letting it drop to the ground. She does not like tomatoes. She'll accept a nut, if she manages to split it into halves with her side teeth, and then she'll chew it carefully. All carrot ends are for her. She takes the stems of broccoli and asparagus and holds them gently, gazing at me for a moment to see if anything else is coming her way before walking to the rug to settle down for a gnaw.

A dog is an animal—this is obviously true. But it isn't the whole story.

A dog is a *domesticated* animal, an animal that lives with

human beings. The word "domesticated" grew from a root word that means "belonging to the house." Dogs are animals who belong around houses, animals who have been changed, by years and years of breeding, to live easily and comfortably inside a human home.

To understand what a dog is about we have to understand where he came from, and how he became an animal that belongs to a house. The domestic dog is distantly related to coyotes and jackals and foxes, dingoes and dholes (a wild dog with reddish fur that lives in Asia). But the ancestors of all dogs today were likely animals most similar to today's gray wolf.

When I see Pumpernickel delicately spit out a tomato, I am certainly not reminded of wolves in Wyoming pulling down a moose and tearing it apart. How did dogs go from being wild hunters to creatures who will wait patiently at the kitchen door for a carrot?

We made them that way.

HOW TO MAKE A DOG

It was our ancestors who created dogs. They did it by choosing animals with traits that they wanted. Traits can be the way an animal looks or acts: its size, strength, intelligence, how easy it is to tame, and so on. The curl of a poodle's coat is a trait, and so is a Labrador retriever's fondness for bringing a ball back to your feet.

Our ancestors made sure that the animals with the

traits they liked mated and had puppies who would carry on those traits. It's called domestication, this process of changing a wild animal into a tame one that suits the needs of humans. What your dog looks like, how he acts, how much interest he shows in you, how he pays attention to what *you* are paying attention to: These all happened because of domestication.

So how do you make a dog? There are just a few ingredients. You'll need wolves, humans, a little interaction, and patience on both sides. Mix thoroughly and wait, oh, a few thousand years.

One scientist tried it. Dmitri Belyaev found a group of captive silver foxes and started carefully breeding them, selecting the traits he wanted to see carried on from parent to pup. In Siberia in the 1950s, the silver fox was a small, wild animal that had become popular for its fur. They were kept in pens, captive but not tame. Belyaev started with a group of 130 silver foxes. He chose and bred those that were the least aggressive or fearful around people.

Belyaev came up to each caged fox and offered it food out of his hand. Some bit at him; some hid. Some took the food, reluctantly. These foxes were allowed to mate, and their puppies were tested in the same way. When the tamest of their puppies were old enough, they were mated as well. Over time, some foxes took the food and let themselves be touched and petted without fleeing or snarling. Still others took the food and even wagged and whimpered at the scientist, asking for more interaction. They seemed, by nature, to be calmer around people— even interested in them.

After forty years of this careful breeding, three quarters of the foxes could be called domesticated. They did not just accept or tolerate contact with people; they seemed to be drawn toward it. They would whimper to attract attention. They sniffed and licked humans, much as dogs do. Belyaev had created a domesticated fox.

Later testing showed that the bred foxes had different genes than their wild cousins. (Genes are the instructions inside cells for building a certain kind of living creature. A fox has a certain set of genes; a dog another; a human being or a pine tree, still another.) This meant that by breeding the animals for tameness, Belyaev had actually created a different animal. Along with the new genes came a new and different look. Some of the later foxes had spotted or mottled fur, much like mixed-breed dogs everywhere. Their ears flopped rather than stood straight up; their tails curled up and over their backs. Their heads were wider and their muzzles shorter than other foxes. The domesticated foxes looked, in fact, more like dogs.

Something very similar to Belyaev's experiment probably happened with wolves many centuries ago. To understand dogs today, we must first try to understand the wolves that they came from.

Wolves can be found in environments from deserts to

forest to ice. For the most part, wolves live in packs. Each pack has one pair of parents, and these two mate and produce puppies. The pack also has anywhere from four to forty younger wolves, usually related to the mated pair. The pack cooperates, sharing tasks. Older wolves may help raise the pups, and the whole group works together when hunting large prey. Wolves are very territorial, and spend a good amount of time marking and defending their borders, making sure that other wolves stay out of the area where they live.

At some time early in human history, wolves and people began to interact. Some scientists have suggested this story: As human beings gathered in settled villages and communities, they produced garbage that piled up nearby. Wolves, who scavenge dead food as well as hunting live animals, would have quickly discovered this new source of meals. The boldest among them may have overcome their fear of the strange, furless human animals and begun feasting on their scrap pile.

Generation after generation of wolves who were not too afraid of people would have more and more success living on the edge of human villages. Slowly, they became more scavengers than hunters. Over time, people began to take a few pups in as pets. They would have bred the animals they particularly liked. This was the first step of domestication.

We know that truly domesticated wolf-dogs existed

between ten and fourteen thousand years ago. Dog remains have been found in trash heaps and also in graves, their skeletons curled up next to human skeletons. There were probably dogs living with or near humans even earlier than this, although it hasn't yet been proven for certain. Dogs and people may have been together for tens of thousands of years. Or hundreds of thousands.

In some ways, these early dogs—though they were already becoming domesticated—would have thought and acted like their wolf ancestors. And wolves do not (usually) live alone. The life of a wolf is bound up with being part of a pack. When early dogs came to live with humans, they brought some of the instincts and skills of pack living with them.

Wolf pups are born into packs, but only stay until they are a few years old. Then they leave. They may find a mate and create a new pack, or they may join a different pack that already exists. The flexibility that lets a young wolf adapt to different packmates helped early dogs adjust to life with human beings.

Life in a pack also means that a wolf must pay attention to what other wolves are doing. Similarly, early dogs needed to keep an eye on their human keepers, to stay aware of what the people were doing. Watchful, adaptable, and skilled at paying attention to what others were doing, early dogs settled into their lives with people. And that was when things started to *really* change.

UNWOLFY

Dogs came from wolves and are similar to wolves—but they are not wolves. The ways wolves and dogs are different show how domestication changed one kind of animal into another.

Some of the differences between dogs and wolves show up early. Wolf pups open their eyes at ten days old; dog puppies do not open their eyes for two or more weeks. Generally, puppies are slower than wolf pups to develop into adults. Learning to walk, carrying objects in their mouths, beginning to play biting games—these are all things that happen later for dog puppies than wolf pups.

These may seem like small differences, but they actually have a large effect on how dogs grow up. Dogs are puppies for longer than wolves. They have more time to learn how to behave around other animals.

In his first few months, a puppy learns much about the other creatures around him. He sorts out who is a dog, an ally, or a stranger. If young puppies spend time with animals that are not dogs—humans or monkeys or rabbits or cats—they form an "attachment" to those species, meaning that as adults, they will prefer those kinds of animals. A dog who spends early time with humans will grow up comfortable in the company of humans.

This comfort with animals who are not dogs is part of what makes a dog a dog, and not a wolf.

There is more.

Dogs do not form true packs, as wolves do. If they need to find their own food, dogs will scavenge or hunt small prey. They may hunt with another dog nearby, but the two dogs will not hunt as a team to bring down prey.

A dog learns early on who his most important care-taker is, and forms a special attachment to that person or persons. Dogs may become anxious when their people are away, and greet them with special excitement when they come back. Wolves greet other members of the pack on return, but they do not single out one packmate for partic-ular greeting. Life in a pack means that attachment to all packmates makes the most sense. Life with human beings means that attachment to a person works best.

Dogs and wolves are different physically. Wolves who live in a similar environment are roughly the same size and shape, while dogs can range from the four-pound papillon to the two-hundred-pound Newfoundland. And yet they are all dogs. The dog's skin is also thicker than the wolf's, and his teeth are smaller. A dog's head is smaller too, and so is the brain inside it.

Does this mean that wolves, with a bigger brain, are smarter? Not necessarily. Scientists once thought that ani-mals with bigger brains were more intelligent, but that idea is no longer considered always true. It's more import-ant to look at what that brain can *do*.

Tests that compare the intelligence of wolves and dogs have shown some differences between them. But it is important to take a careful look at these differences to see what they really mean.

There are certain kinds of problems that wolves seem to solve more easily than dogs. Wolves are great at escaping from closed cages. Most dogs are not. Researchers tested wolves and dogs by seeing how long it took them to learn a task—to pull three ropes in a particular order. Wolves outperformed the dogs every time.

So are the wolves smarter?

In some ways: Wolves are definitely better at solving certain physical problems—ones that involve objects (like ropes). In their natural life, wolves spend more time grabbing and pulling on things (like struggling prey) than dogs do. Pulling on a rope is not a skill that most dogs need in their daily life.

In another way, though, dogs excel: in understanding people. As we will see, dogs are good at getting people to solve their tasks for them.

And there is one final, critical difference between wolves and dogs. It seems very small, but it makes a huge difference. Here it is:

Dogs look at our eyes.

Dogs make eye contact and look to people for information. They study us to figure out where the food is, what we are feeling, and what is happening. Wolves—like most animals—stay away from eye contact. If one wolf stares at another, it is a threat.

ALEXANDRA HOROWITZ

Most dogs will turn away from a stare if it goes on too long. But, unlike wolves, they seem to want to inspect our faces. They look up at us for information, for reassurance, for guidance. This is pleasing to us—there's something satisfying in gazing at a dog who is gazing back at you. But it also comes with a direct benefit to the dog. This habit of paying attention to people helps dogs get along with us.

Perhaps eye contact was actually the first step in that process of domestication that turned wolves into dogs. Maybe people, long ago, chose the animals that looked back at them.

Once people had taken dogs into their homes, we began to do something peculiar with them. We began designing them.

FANCY DOGS

The label on her cage said LAB MIX. Every dog in the shelter was a Lab mix. But at first I thought Pump, with her black silky hair and her velvet ears, was surely born of a spaniel. In sleep she was a perfect bear cub. Soon her tail hairs grew longer and feathery. So she's a golden retriever. As she aged, her belly grew until she had a solid, barrel-like shape. So she's a Lab after all. Her tail became a flag that needed trimming—a Lab/golden mix. She could be

still one moment and sprinting the next—a
poodle. She's her own dog.

By carefully choosing which dogs to breed, human beings
have created dogs of all kinds. Dogs vary in shape, size, lifetime, temperament, and skills. The outgoing Norwich terrier, ten pounds and ten inches high, is the same weight as
the head of a calm, sweet, enormous Newfoundland. Ask
some dogs to fetch a ball and all you get is a puzzled look,
but a border collie doesn't have to be asked twice.

Human beings began creating different breeds of dogs
at least five thousand years ago. In drawings from ancient
Egypt you can see at least two kinds of dogs. Some look
like mastiffs, big of head and body. Others are slim with
curly tails. The big dogs may have been guard dogs, the
smaller ones hunters. And so we started designing dogs
for our own purposes.

By the sixteenth century we had hounds, bird dogs,
terriers, and shepherds. By the nineteenth century, breed
clubs were formed and dog shows began judging dogs,
choosing the best examples of many breeds.

The American Kennel Club now lists nearly 150
breeds. To be a member of a breed—a purebred—a dog
must have a mother and father who were members of that
breed. Purebred dogs look much like their mothers and
fathers. They are also more vulnerable to certain physical
problems and illnesses than mixed-breed dogs.

Dogs of one breed are different from dogs of another in size and shape of body and head, type of tail, length of fur, and color of coat. Some people say that purebred dogs are different not just in looks, but in *who they are* as well. Go searching for a purebred dog and you'll find books and people who will tell you not only what your dog is supposed to look like, but what they claim he'll *be* like. Want a long-legged, short-haired, jowly dog? Think about the Great Dane. In more of a mood for a short-nosed, rolled-skin, curly-tail dog? Here's a nice pug for you. An English cocker spaniel is advertised as being "merry and affectionate"; a chow chow as "distant and reserved with strangers"; a shar-pei is thought to be "dignified, lordly, scowling, sober, and snobbish."

But it is not so simple. Dogs, like human beings, are more than their ancestry. They are not simple carbon copies of their parents. Each dog is different at birth, and each dog will lead his own life. How the dog is raised and treated, what the dog experiences, and who he meets, will shape who the dog becomes. This is as important, or even more important, than what the dog inherits from his parents.

But there is one difference between breeds that is worth remembering.

Purebred dogs tend to react in a certain way to something that catches their interest—say, a running rabbit or a bird taking flight. Breeds that have been used for hunting (such as spaniels, retrievers, or pointers) have, over the years, come to react strongly to the movement of an animal that looks like prey. Most dogs will notice a small fleeing animal. A hunting dog will not just notice it. He will react to it. And he will be more likely to chase it than, say, a shih tzu or a pug.

In the same way, dogs who were bred to be herders (think of border collies) tend to react in a certain way to groups of sheep, people, ducks, or squirrels: they try to corral them into a group. These dogs do not know that they are supposed to herd. But they notice the way individuals and groups move. If one sheep (or one squirrel, or one child) tries to leave the group, a herder is likely to go after it and try to make it return.

Knowing the breed of a dog can give you an idea of how he might act before you even meet him. But it is a mistake to think that knowing the breed means you know *all* about the dog. What you really know is that the dog will probably have certain tendencies—to chase things that move quickly, say. A breed name like "Labrador retriever" or "toy poodle" is a beginning, not an ending, of what can be known about a dog. And the breed by itself doesn't tell us much about the dog's *umwelt*—about what it *feels like* to be that dog. That is what we are going to try to discover.

ANIMALS WITH SOMETHING EXTRA

It's snowing and the sun is rising, which means
we have about three minutes for me to get dressed

ALEXANDRA HOROWITZ

and get us into the park to play before the snow is trampled. Outside, I plow clumsily through the deep snow, and Pump hurtles through it with great bounds. I plop down to make a snow angel, and Pump throws herself down beside me. She seems to be making a snow-dog angel, twisting to and fro on her back. I look to her with complete joy at our shared play. Then I smell a horrible odor coming from her direction. Pump is not making a snow-dog angel; she's rolling in the rotting carcass of a small, dead animal.

Some people think of dogs—no matter the breed—as wild animals at their core. This group tends to explain dog behavior by referring back to wolf behavior. Others think of dogs as something human beings have entirely created. This is a group that tends to treat dogs as four-footed, slobbery people.

Neither group is correct. The answer is right in the middle. Dogs are animals, of course, with wolfish roots, but if we stop here we won't get a complete picture of the dog. Dogs are not wolves anymore; they have been changed. Now they are animals with something extra added. They are animals but not quite the animals they once were.

For instance, let's take a closer look at the false idea that dogs see us as their "pack." Very frequently human beings talk about the dog-and-human family as a pack. They say that the human should be the head of the pack, the "dominant" one. It's an idea that comes from thinking of dogs as wolves. Dogs came from wolflike ancestors; wolves form packs; therefore dogs feel like they live in packs with dominant humans.

The idea of a human-dog pack first seems sensible, and it gives us a way to think about our lives with dogs, if we are unsure. In this conception, people are dominant; dogs should be submissive. We command, the dog obeys. We walk the dog; the dog doesn't walk us.

But this idea is not true. It starts with a mistake. In the wild, a wolf pack is not a simple matter of a single commander and many followers. Wolf packs are families; almost all members are related. A typical pack is made up of a male and female pair—the "alphas"—and some of their children. Only the alpha pair mates. Everyone cooperates to raise the pups. Different wolves hunt and share food. Many packmates come together to hunt large prey, which would be too big for any single wolf.

It makes more sense to look at the pack's breeding pair as parents, rather than rulers. They are in charge because they are the oldest, just as human parents are in charge of a family. Older wolves are often dominant, and younger wolves are more submissive; this is true. But submissive wolves do not scramble for power or try to become alphas themselves. Instead, wolves use dominant and submissive behavior to keep the pack together.

A young wolf will approach an older wolf with a low wagging tail and a body close to the ground. The younger wolf is acknowledging an elder, accepting that the older wolf has a higher rank in the pack. Pups are not usually put in their place by older wolves. They simply learn how to act by interacting with and observing their packmates.

For dogs, things are different.

In the first place, dogs do *not* usually live in the kinds of packs wolves do. Even stray, free-ranging dogs who may never have lived in a human family do not form packs as wolves do. And the lives of dogs who do live with a human family do not much resemble the lives of wolves in packs.

A wolf pack is constantly changing. Pups are born. Young wolves grow up and leave. The size and membership of the pack changes with the years, the seasons, with how much prey is around to be hunted. But dogs adopted by a human family live a stable life. No one is pushed out of the house in the spring or joins up just for the big winter moose hunt.

So a dog living with humans is not living in a pack. But he *is* living in a family. Like other families, people and dogs share habits, preferences, home. We sleep together and rise together. We walk the same routes and even stop to greet the same dogs. Our dog-and-human family works because we share basic rules of behavior.

For example, the humans in the family all agree that nobody is to urinate on the living room rug. When a dog enters the family, he needs to be taught that this is one of the ways his new family behaves. If a dog trainer has an idea that a human-and-dog family is like a wolf pack, and that the alpha pair in a pack are strict enforcers of the rules, he'll insist that a dog be punished for peeing on the rug—with a yell, forcing the dog down, a sharp word, a jerk on the collar.

But this is *not* how things would happen in an actual wolf pack, even if the alpha pair did have strange rules about urination. Wolves seem to learn not by punishing one another but by watching one another. Dogs are also keen observers of their humans. They'll learn best if you let them discover for themselves what behaviors are rewarded and what are simply ignored.

Your relationship with your dog will be shaped by what happens when your dog does something you do not like— such as the moment you come home to discover a puddle on the floor. Punishing the dog for this (which may have happened hours ago) is a quick way to make your relationship

ALEXANDRA HOROWITZ

all about bullying. The result will be a dog who becomes extra sensitive and possibly fearful, but not one who understands that, in this family, we don't pee on the rug.

Dogs are not pack animals, not in the same way wolves are. But they *have* inherited something important from their wolflike ancestors—an interest in being around others and in paying attention to what those others are doing. Wolves would not succeed in pack life without this skill. Dogs use this same skill to succeed in life with a human family.

Let your dog use his skills at watching you. Behavior that his family doesn't like gets no attention, no food— nothing that your dog wants from you. Good behavior gets it all. And you, watch the dog. Look for the signs he gives you that he is about to pee, and take him to a good place to do it. He'll learn from you. That is how the dog-human group can turn itself into a family.

But animals with something extra are still animals. Every now and then, we see snatches of the ancient wolf in our pets. You may glimpse a growl when you move to take a beloved ball from your dog's mouth. You might watch rough-and-tumble play in which one animal seems more like prey than playmate, or see a glimmer of wildness in the eye of a dog grabbing for a meat bone.

This unpredictable, wild side of dogs is real. The ancestors of dogs were predators. Their jaws are strong, their teeth are made for tearing meat. They act without pausing to think. They have an urge to protect—themselves, their families, their home—and we cannot always predict what they will see as a threat.

Living with a family member who is not a wolf, but is still an animal, is a process of learning. The first time your dog tears from your side, running wildly off the trail after some invisible thing in the bushes, you panic. With time, you and the dog will both become more used to each other. Your dog will learn about trails, and that he is expected to stay on (or at least near) them. You may never learn to see invisible things in bushes, but after a dozen walks, you'll learn that there *are* things in bushes, that your dog loves to chase them, and that he will return to you.

Your dog is not a wild animal, a wolf with poodle's curls. Nor is he a human being covered in fur. He's an animal with something extra, an animal changed by thousands of years of living with people.

MAKING YOUR DOG

As you choose a new dog from among a litter of pups or a loud shelter of barking mutts and bring him home, you begin to "make a dog." It's a little like starting that long history of domestication all over again.

Each time you pet your dog, or speak to your dog, or teach your dog, you are explaining his new world—with you—to him. No dog knows, when he first sees the person peeking into his shelter cage, what that person expects of him.

Most of us want similar things from our dogs. Be friendly, loyal, pettable. Find me charming and lovable, but know that I am in charge. Do not pee in the house. Do not jump on guests. Do not chew my shoes. Do not get into the trash.

Dogs aren't born knowing these things. Each dog has to be taught that this is what life with people will mean.

The dogs learns, through you, the kinds of things that are important to you. As you and your dog play and walk and sit and think together, the dog will become *your* dog—interested in your comings and goings, paying attention to you, playful at just the right times. Your dog will figure out his world—your world—by acting and by watching others act.

The more time that you and your dog spend together, the more you will make your dog into who he was meant to be—a member of a dog-and-human family.

3

SNIFF

First Sniff of the Day: Pump wanders into the living room in the morning while I am dishing out her food. She's looking sleepy, but her nose is wide awake, stretching every which way as though doing its morning exercises. She reaches her nose toward the food without moving her body, and sniffs. A look at me. Another sniff. She's made up her mind about the food I've offered her, and she backs away from the bowl. Then she forgives me by nosing my hand. We go outside, and now her nose is almost dancing, happily taking in smells that float by on the air.

We humans don't tend to spend a lot of time thinking about smelling. Smells are just minor blips compared to all the things that we see. The room you're in right now is a wild mix of colors and textures, of small movements, of shadows and lights. If you really call your attention to it, maybe you can smell a chocolate brownie on the table next to you, or perhaps the fresh scent of this book when it's cracked open—but only if you bury your nose in its pages.

If we *do* notice a smell, it's usually because we have a feeling about that smell. Hot cinnamon buns smell wonderful; month-old garbage smells awful. But most of the time, we don't notice smells simply as sources of information. And it's taken us a long time to come to understand how different things are for animals like dogs, who live by their noses.

The things we're starting to find out now are incredibly surprising. As we *see* the world, a dog *smells* it. The dog's universe is a fascinating place of odors, one on top of the other. The world of scents is at least as rich a place as the world of sights.

Pumpernickel has her tracking-something-interesting sniff, with her nose deep in a patch of good grass. She has her checking-this-out sniff, judging a hand held out to her. She has her alarm-clock sniff, close enough to my sleeping face to tickle me with her whiskers. And she has her thoughtful sniff, nose held high in a breeze. All are followed by a half sneeze—just the *choo*, no *ah*—as if to clear her nose for the next smell.

Every one of these sniffs gives Pumpernickel an astonishing amount of information about her world.

Dogs don't take objects in their hands to figure them out. They don't stare at them to understand them. They don't point and ask someone else to explain what that thing might be.

Instead they walk bravely up to a new, unknown object, stretch their magnificent snouts within millimeters of it, and take a nice deep sniff.

Go ahead, take a sniff yourself. As you do so, and then exhale, the smells that have entered your nose are pushed right back out. Dogs have a way to avoid this. They breathe in through the nostrils, as you do, but then they exhale through the tiny slits on the side of their nostrils—you can see them if you look closely at the dog's nose. This way, they can keep sniffing odors *in* without sending those odors *out*.

Each sniff begins with muscles in the nostrils straining to draw a current of air inside. Once the air has been vacuumed in, it encounters a lot of nose. Most dogs have long muzzles, with lots of room for channels lined with cells that are sensitive to the smells being drawn in from the outside air.

Once a smell is drawn into the nose, it touches tiny, specialized spots called receptor sites. From there, information is sent in bursts to the dog's brain. Information from the nose reaches the brain even more quickly than information from the ears or the eyes. And a lot of a dog's brain is dedicated to understanding what the nose is telling it. About one eighth of a dog's brain works to process smells; that is more than the percentage of the human brain that works to process sight.

Human noses have about six million receptor sites; sheepdog noses, over two hundred million; beagle noses, over three hundred million. This means that a beagle's sense of smell may be *millions* of times more sensitive than a human's. Next to dogs, we smell almost nothing. We might notice if a teaspoon of sugar is stirred into our iced tea; a dog can detect of teaspoon of sugar stirred into a million gallons of water: two Olympic-sized pools full!

And dogs actually have what I like to call a "second" nose. It is called the vomeronasal organ, and it is a specialized sac above the roof of the mouth, below the floor of the nose. It is covered with more receptor sites, giving a dog even more chances to discover his world by smell. (Other animals have vomeronasal organs too. A snake or lizard that darts its tongue out is not trying to taste something; it is using the tongue to bring a smell to its vomeronasal organ.)

The vomeronasal organ is particularly useful in helping the dog smell pheromones. These are chemicals that, when released by animals, give information about each animal's physical state, such as whether they are ready to mate.

Pheromones are often carried in a fluid, such as urine. If you're a close observer of dogs, you will have noticed that they are interested in the urine of other dogs. Extremely interested. So interested that they . . . wait, gross! Stop licking that! Dogs may well lick up the urine of other dogs, especially if one of those dogs is a female interested in mating. Licking may bring the urine right up to the vomeronasal organ for careful investigation.

The tongue isn't the only path for chemicals like pheromones to get to this organ. A nice moist nose works too: This is one reason dogs have wet noses. Odors from the air have a hard time reaching the vomeronasal organ, tucked as it is inside the mouth. When a dog gives something interesting (say, the skin of your hand after you've been gone for a while) a hearty sniff, invisible bits of that skin stick to the wet surface of the dog's nose. From there, they can dissolve and travel to the vomeronasal organ. When your dog nuzzles against you, he is actually collecting your odor on his nose, all the better to be sure that you're you.

What is it like to have a sense of smell like a dog's? It's hard for us to imagine, but think for a minute about your sense of sight. If you looked closely at a rose, you might see traces of pollen, a damaged leaf, a dewdrop on a thorn, a petal going dry and brown. Now imagine that every detail you can see has, to a dog, its own particular smell. A dog, sniffing that same rose, can *smell* the pollen from faraway flowers; can smell a burst of chemicals where a leaf is torn; the dampness of a dewdrop; and even the odor of decay as a petal starts to die.

Dogs can also smell things that are invisible to our sight. We can only *see* the rose in a single moment in time, but a dog can *smell* the rose's past—as well as its present. Through his nose, a dog can actually know who has held that rose—and when they held it. For dogs, smell tells time. Odors weaken over time, so the strength of a smell tells a dog that it is recent; if the smell is not so strong, it's older. When dogs smell odors that have faded, they are smelling things that have happened in the past. Even the future can be smelled—on the breeze that brings air from the place you and your dog are headed together.

SMELLING A PERSON

What does the world look like from the point of view of a nose? Let's start with what they smell all the time: us and each other.

Humans stink. The human armpit is one of the smelliest places on any animal. Our breath is a confusion of smell after smell. Our skin is covered with sweat and oil that hold our own particular scent. When we touch something, we leave a bit of ourselves on it—an invisible smear made up of tiny pieces of skin. This is "our smell."

If we touch something soft—a slipper, say—and we

spend a lot of time touching it, it will become a part of us to a creature of the nose. For your dog, your slipper is a part of you. To us, the slipper may not look like something that would be terribly interesting, but anyone who has returned home to find a slipper chewed to bits knows better.

We don't even need to touch objects for them to smell like us. As we move, we leave behind a trail of skin cells. The air is perfumed with our dried sweat. Added to this, we smell of what we've eaten today, whom we've kissed, what we've brushed against. Whatever perfume we've put on merely adds to the medley. As a result, our dogs find it incredibly easy to tell who we are by our scent alone. Trained dogs can tell identical twins apart by scent.

To dogs, we *are* our scent. They recognize us with their noses much as we recognize our friends by sight.

ALEXANDRA HOROWITZ

When we come home at the end of the day, dogs typically greet our fascinating mixed-up smell promptly and lovingly. If you were to come home drenched in a new perfume or wearing someone else's clothes, your dogs might be puzzled for a moment—you would not seem like yourself. But your natural scent would soon give you away.

Dogs are not the only animals who "see" with scent. Sharks have been observed following the same zigzaggy path through the water that an injured fish took some time before. Through both its blood and the chemicals it leaves behind, the fish has left a bit of itself behind for the shark to track. But dogs are unique in one way: They are the only animals both trained and bred to use scent to follow someone who is long gone.

Bloodhounds are one of the supersmellers among dogs. They have more nose tissue—more *nose*—than most dogs. Many other features of their bodies also help them to smell extra well. Their ears are terrifically long, but this isn't to make them hear better. Instead, a slight swing of the head sets these ears in motion, fanning up more scented air for the nose to catch. Their constant stream of drool is also a perfect way for the dog to gather up smells in the air and bring them to the vomeronasal organ.

Basset hounds (which are thought to be bred from bloodhounds) go a step further. Their short legs mean that their whole head is already at ground—or scent—level.

These hounds are naturally good at smelling. They can also be trained to pay attention to certain scents and ignore others. In this way, they can follow a scent left by a person who has passed by a day earlier, or even many days before. They can even let a human handler know when two people who were walking together have gone separate ways.

Hounds track not just by noticing odors, but by noticing very small changes in odors. With every second that passes, a smell left on the ground (say, in a footprint made by someone running) gets weaker. A trained tracking dog can tell which footprints smell stronger and which smell less so, and by doing so can tell which way a person was running. This is very handy for tracking a criminal, for example, or someone who is lost and in need of rescue.

Maybe you're not fleeing a crime scene or lost in the wilderness, but there are other reasons to respect how well a dog can smell you. Dogs can do more than simply smell that you are you. They can also smell what you have been doing and how you are feeling.

A dog can tell if you've just hugged a friend or had a snack or run a mile. And if you're sad or worried or afraid, your dog can likely smell this as well. This isn't a magical ability on the part of your dog. Fear has a smell. A real one.

When you are afraid, your body changes. Your heart speeds up. So does your breathing. You sweat more. Your body produces adrenaline, a chemical that gives you extra strength for running away or for fighting off an attacker.

And your body releases more of those chemicals known as pheromones.

Researchers have shown that many social animals, from bees to deer, can sense pheromones when another animal of their species is frightened or harmed. Once they sense these pheromones, the animals take action to get themselves to safety. In the same way, your dog can smell the changes that fear makes in your body. Your dog probably notices other changes too, in the way you stand and walk and speak. So chances are, if you've got the heebie-jeebies, your dog knows it.

Your dog may also know if you have something else—a disease.

Even human doctors have noticed that patients with certain diseases smell a certain way. A person with typhoid fever smells of freshly baked bread; someone with tuberculosis will breathe out air with a stale, sour scent. And these doctors only have human noses. Imagine what a dog might be able to detect!

Researchers have begun training dogs to recognize a particular smell—one produced by cancer tissue. (Cancer is a disease that causes cells in the body to start multiplying, often creating tumors.) Although the number of trained dogs is small, the results are impressive. In one study, the dogs made 1,272 attempts to detect which patients had cancer—and missed only fourteen times. In another experiment, they sniffed out the cancer every time.

Does this mean that your dog will let you know if someone in your family has cancer? Probably not, since your dog hasn't been trained to identify that particular smell. What these studies reveal is that dogs have the ability to smell changes in a person's health—and this is just the tip of the iceberg.

SMELLING A DOG

A dog can smell who a person is, where that person has been, and how that person feels, even without the person making any special effort to let the dog know these things. When it comes to smelling another dog, however, things are different. Dogs leave their scent behind on purpose for other dogs to find. They communicate with smell.

All members of the dog family—dogs, wolves, foxes, coyotes, and others—leave urine conspicuously splashed on all kinds of objects. This is called urine marking, and it carries a message; it's a note left by one dog's rear end to be discovered by another dog's front end.

Urine isn't the only calling card a dog leaves. Feces, or solid waste, also holds informative odors, not only from the stuff itself but also from small organs near the tail. These are called anal glands and they release an extremely foul smell—think dead-fish-in-a-sweatsock. This stench is different for each individual dog. (Anal glands also let loose their contents when a dog is afraid or alarmed; veterinary offices sometimes smell of them.)

On top of this, your dog may scratch at the ground after he's left urine or feces. It's not to cover up what they have done; why would they want to cover up something so interesting? Instead, scratching may add new odors from the pads of the paws, or it may offer a visual hint to other dogs, leading them to the place where it will be most informative to take a good deep sniff. On a windy day, dogs may seem friskier, more likely to scratch the ground. They could be leading other dogs to a message that could quickly drift away on the breeze if not smelled soon.

Dogs seem to delight in smelling other dogs. Humans don't always feel the same way about the smell that comes from our furry companions. When a dog smells like a dog, we tend to want to give him a bath.

A well-walked dog who's had a glorious day of play can definitely spread dirt around. But we take something away from our dogs when we are too quick to give them baths, not to mention scrubbing our houses to perfection. What smells clean to a human nose is actually the smell of soap or detergent—a fragrance that must insult a dog's sensitive nose.

A dog will prefer it if we keep the occasional well-worn T-shirt around and don't scrub the floors for a while. No dog has the natural desire to be what we would call clean. It is no wonder that a dog follows a bath by hightailing it to roll vigorously on the rug or in the grass. He wants to smell like something again, to feel more like himself.

THE SMELL OF THE DOG'S WORLD

Thinking about smell helps us to understand a dog's world, his *umwelt*. To get there, we must think of objects, people, emotions, even times of day, as having their own particular smells.

I used to be fooled by Pump's motionless posture when we sat outside together. I thought she was doing nothing. Then, one time, looking more closely at her, I saw that she was motionless except for one part: her nostrils. They were churning information through their channels, gathering up all the smells before her.

What was she "seeing" with her nose? The unknown

dog who just turned the corner of the block? A barbecue down the hill? An approaching storm? The doggy smell, the grilled meat, even the wind sweeping the storm our way are all things her nose can pick up.

Whatever Pump was doing, she was definitely not being lazy. She was busy. She was smelling.

Knowing how important smell is to a dog changed the way I thought about what Pump was doing. Now I understood that not allowing her to sniff visitors at the door is the same as blindfolding myself as I open the door to a stranger. I began to ask my guests to kneel and hold out their hands for her nose, or to let their heads or bodies be sniffed. I even started to see why Pump, and maybe your dog as well, is so keen on sticking her nose in places that seem, well, pretty inappropriate. Those places, to a dog, are marvelously smelly. No human wants a dog's nose there, but the dog is simply trying to "see," with her nose, who you are.

In the same way, I would never scold a dog for greeting a newcomer dog to the neighborhood by smelling his rump. Rump-sniffing seems unpleasant to humans, but this doesn't matter to dogs. For dogs, by all means, the closer the better. If one dog doesn't want his rump sniffed, he will let the other dogs know. Humans who try to stop this exchange of extremely fascinating smells will only get both dogs worked up.

Since I've begun to appreciate Pump's smelly world, I sometimes take her out just to sit and sniff. We have "smell walks," stopping at every landmark in which she expresses an interest. She is *looking*. Being outside is the most smelly, wonderful part of her day. I won't cut that short.

But I'm happiest of all to be greeted by her sniff when I come in the door, followed by her wag of recognition. I nuzzle into the scruff of her neck and sniff her right back.

DOG TALK

Pump sits close to me and quietly pants, gazing at me: She wants something. On our walks she hops up, swings around on her rear legs, and heads back the way we came to tell me when we've gone far enough. I turn on the bathwater and turn to her with a smile. Her tail drops and wags low, her ears flattening to her head. All this talking and yet no words at all.

Dogs never respond in words when we speak to them. Like most animals, however, they are not silent, and it is not hard for them to communicate.

Like wolves, dogs communicate with their eyes, ears, tail, and the ways they hold their bodies. They squeal, growl, grunt, yelp, moan, whine, whimper, bark, yawn, and howl. And that's just in the first few weeks.

Dogs talk. This comes as no surprise to most dog owners. What *is* surprising is how often they are communicating, and in how many ways. They talk to each other, they talk to you, and they talk to noises that are on the other side of closed doors or hidden in high grasses.

Dogs communicate for the same reasons people do— because they, and we, are social animals, living closely with others. Members of the dog family who do not live in groups, such as foxes, do not seem to have as much to say. Even the kinds of sounds foxes make reflect the fact that they live alone: They make loud sounds that travel well over long distances.

Dogs sometimes do this too, but they can also make sounds meant to be heard by someone close enough to touch. Dogs whisper as well as bellow. And if we know how to listen, we will be able to hear what they have to say.

OUT LOUD

Imagine a park on a warm spring day.

Two human beings stroll along, chatting. They discuss the warmth of the air, and the nature of other human beings. They express love for each other. One warns the other to watch out for the tree straight ahead. They do all of this by making small, strange contortions of their mouths, placing their tongues in various positions, and squeezing air from their lungs.

This is not the only communication going on.

As the human beings walk, the two dogs by their sides may scold each other, confirm their friendship, court each other, claim ownership of a stick, or announce loyalty to a particular person.

Humans communicate with complicated, symbolic language. No other animal uses anything quite like it. But we sometimes forget than even creatures who do not use spoken words may be talking up a storm.

Instead of words, animals have whole other systems of behavior that get information from a sender (speaker) to someone on the receiving end (listener). Animal communication can take place through body language—using limbs, heads, eyes, tails, or the entire body—or even through such surprising forms as changing skin color, urinating, leaving solid waste behind, or trying to appear larger or smaller.

Birds twitter, peep, and sing songs. Humpback whales sing too. Bats make high-pitched clicks; elephants rumble. The wiggling dance of a honeybee tells another bee where food is, how long it will take to get there, and how good that food seems to be. A monkey's yawn is a threat. A firefly's flashes tell what species it is. A poison dart frog's color announces just how poisonous it is.

All of these things are communication. How do we know? We can spot a communication by noticing if one animal changes its behavior after another animal makes a noise or performs an action. If so, it's probably safe to decide that something has been said.

The communication that is easiest for us to notice is the one that is most similar to our own: communication out loud.

WHAT DOGS HEAR

Thunder outside. Pump's ears, velvet triangles that fold perfectly along the side of her head, prick up. Head up, eyes to the window, she identifies the sound: a storm, a frightening thing. Her ears pivot back, flattened along her skull. I coo to her to comfort her and watch her ears for feedback. The tips soften but she relaxes them only slightly, still holding her ears against her head as if to shut out the thunder's roar.

Dogs' ears come in dazzling variety: extremely long, small and perked, folding gracefully alongside the face. They can be triangular or round, floppy or upright. In most dogs, the outer part of the ear moves to allow sound to travel more easily to the inner ear.

ALEXANDRA HOROWITZ

Dogs' ears have evolved to hear certain kinds of sounds. So have ours. The pitch of a sound (how high or low it is) can be measured in units called hertz. A high-pitched squeal has many hertz, a low rumble has few. Human ears can hear a range of about twenty hertz (the lowest moan from the longest organ pipe) to twenty thousand hertz (the highest squeaky squeak).

Dogs hear most of what we hear and then some. They can detect sounds up to forty-five thousand hertz, much higher than our ears can pick up. (This is where the power of the dog whistle comes from: It produces a sound too high-pitched for human ears, but easy for dogs to hear.) Even a quiet room is full of noises higher than we can hear. Your digital alarm clock pulses. A fluorescent light hums. Rats running by in the night chirp as they find their way. Termites' bodies vibrate. A dog's ears pick up all these sounds that are silent to us.

Dogs easily hear human voices too. They are nearly as good as we are at noticing changes in pitch. A sentence that ends on a low pitch? A statement. A sentence that ends on a rising pitch? A question (at least in American English). Ask your dog, "Do you want to go for a walk?" and let your voice rise on the final word; if your dog is used to going on walks with you, he'll respond with excitement. Try it without the rise in pitch at the end, and your dog may not even notice the word "walk."

Dogs seem more interested in high-pitched sounds

than in lower ones. They'll come more quickly in response to high-pitched, repeated calls than to calls at a lower pitch. Why? It's likely that high-pitched sounds are similar to a tussle nearby or the shrieking of injured prey—things dogs pay keen attention to. So if your dog doesn't come when you call, don't lower and sharpen your voice. This won't catch his attention, plus the tone tells your dog that you're displeased and punishment might follow—so he won't be likely to come.

On the other hand, if you want your dog to sit, try using a lower-pitched command that drops near the end. This is a tone that might be more likely to help a dog relax.

If dogs understand the way our voices work, does that mean that they understand language? It's a tricky question. Researchers agree that no animal has yet been found to have a language like ours. Human language has many different words that stand for complex ideas. These words can be combined in endless patterns, and there are rules for how to do this combining. Though animals communicate a *lot*, no animal seems to use language as we do.

But even if animals do not create language, perhaps they can understand it—at least some of it.

Do dogs know what we mean when we use a word? Probably not exactly. Try asking your dog if he wants to "go for a walk." Here he does seem to know, and will respond with enthusiasm. The next day, try asking (in the same tone of speech) if he wants to "snow forty locks." You'll likely get the same reaction. Your dog is responding to the sounds that you make and the tone of your voice, not to the meaning of your words.

However, there are a few famous dogs who actually do seem to understand what some words mean. One of them, Rico, a border collie in Germany, can identify over two hundred toys by name. If he is shown an enormous heap of all the toys and balls he has ever seen, he can pull out the single one his owner requests. Even better, Rico can quickly learn a name for a new object. Experimenters put a new toy among familiar ones and asked Rico to get it, using a word they knew he had never heard before (because they had just made it up). "Go get the snark, Rico," they told him. Rico picked out the new toy again and again. He connected the unfamiliar word with the unfamiliar toy— he *named* it. Another border collie, Chaser, knows over a *thousand* words.

Rico and Chaser are not using words the way you or I would, but they seem to be showing that they understand words. The fact that these dogs can do this does not mean all dogs are capable of it. Rico and Chaser might be dog geniuses, or at least unusual in their skill with words. Still, at least one dog can learn what a *snark* is, and that shows that dogs do have the mental ability to understand something about language.

Most dogs are not like Rico and Chaser. (For that

matter, most owners are not like their owners, willing to buy and label hundreds of toys!) Most owners, in fact, grumble that their dogs are not very good listeners.

To be fair, dogs and their relatives do not rely on hearing as the most important sense. Although they can hear a broad range of sounds, they are not terribly good at figuring out where a sound is coming from. They must tilt their heads and move their outer ears to pinpoint the source of a sound. Once they know the general direction of a noise that has caught their attention, they use a sharper sense—vision or smell—to investigate further.

One noise that easily catches a dog's attention is the sound of another dog.

WHAT DOGS SAY

Listen to a bunch of dogs at play. At first all you'll hear is a wild racket. But if you pay closer attention, you'll notice the difference between shouts and cries, yelps and barks, play barks and threatening barks.

Researchers have spent hours listening to animals of all kinds making noise, barking, shouting, cooing, clicking, groaning, and screaming. By doing so, they have discovered certain things about sound signals that are always true, no matter what kind of animal makes them.

An animal's signal expresses something about the world—a discovery such as some tasty food; or a danger, such as a predator nearby. Or the signal expresses something about the signalers—who they are, whether they are ready to mate, their membership in a group, their fear, or their pleasure. And a signal causes a change in the behavior of those who hear it. It may call someone closer, frighten someone away, collect a group together, cause a parent to pay attention to a child or cause a mate to pay attention to a partner.

In the end, all of these purposes for making sounds help an animal and its relatives survive.

What signals, then, are dogs making? What are they saying and how are they saying it?

How is the simple part. Most of the sounds a dog makes come out of his mouth. These sounds might be high or low, soft or loud, short or long, made once or repeated over and over. But from a high-pitched whine to a low growl, from a loud yelp to a soft sigh, from a quick bark to a sudden snap of teeth or a long, drawn-out howl, all come from the dog's mouth.

> She sees I'm almost ready. With her head fixed on the ground between her paws, Pump follows me with her eyes as I cross the room gathering my bag, a book, my keys. I scratch her around the ears and move toward the door. She lifts her head and makes a sound: a plaintive yelp. I freeze. Then I look back. She hurries over, wagging. Okay, then. I guess she'll come with me.

The first dog sound you think of is a bark, but in fact dogs do not bark all day long. Most of their daily noises are *not* barks.

There are high-pitched sounds—cries, squeals, whines, whimpers, yelps, and screams. These happen when the dog is in sudden pain or needs attention. They are some of the first sounds a puppy will make, and they tend to attract the attention of a mother. Deaf and blind, newborn puppies cannot easily find their mothers if they need them. It is easier for them to make noise and let their mothers do the finding.

Not all puppy noises are high-pitched. Puppies also make low *moans* or *grunts*. These don't seem to be signs of pain, but instead a kind of dog purr. Puppies make these noises when they are cuddled close with their mother, littermates, or a human caretaker. The sounds might be made on purpose, or they might just be the result of heavy, slow breathing from a relaxed animal; no one is sure. But on purpose or not, the sounds are communication. They help to strengthen the bond between family members, making them feel close and safe with each other.

You don't need to be told that the rumble of a *growl* and the steady *snarl* are aggressive sounds. Part of what makes them aggressive is their low pitch. A large animal tends to make low sounds; a smaller animal's sounds are higher pitched. (A mouse, for example, is squeakier than an elephant.) So growls and snarls sound like noises that would come out of a large animal. If a dog meets another who might be a threat, he wants to appear to be a big, powerful creature, so he makes a big-dog sound, a low growl. A dog making higher-pitched sounds—whines or squeaks—sounds smaller and less threatening.

Growls may be aggressive, but they are still social sounds, which means they are meant for another animal to hear. Dogs don't usually growl at chairs, boxes, or other nonliving things (unless they have been fooled into thinking one of those things is alive). Growls are also more complex than you might think. The growl from a dog playing tug-of-war may sound fearsome, but it is nothing like the warning snarled by a dog when someone makes a move toward a treasured bone.

If you record a genuine "don't you touch my bone" snarl and play it through a speaker set near an unguarded bone, dogs will leave that bone alone. They won't go near it even if there is no other dog in sight. But if the speaker only lets out play growls or the growls dog use to warn a stranger not to get too close, nearby dogs go ahead and grab the bone. They can tell what each growl means, and how serious a threat each growl makes.

If you live with a hound, you are familiar with the *howl*. Howling seems to be a behavior left over from the days when dogs' ancestors lived in social packs. Wolves howl when separated from their group, when gathered together again, and when the group as a whole sets out to hunt. A wolf howling alone is asking for company; a pack howling together may be a rallying cry (think of a cheer at a football game) or just a celebration of the group. It also has a contagious quality; if wolves hear others howling, they will howl themselves.

Humans produce some contagious sounds too. One of them is the laugh. If you are with a group of laughing friends, chances are you'll soon be laughing too. Do dogs laugh? Well, only when something is terrific fun. Yes, dogs have what has been called a laugh. It is a breathy burst that sounds like excited panting. We could call it *social panting*. Dogs don't seem to produce this sound when they are sitting by themselves. It is only heard when they are playing or are trying to get someone to play with them. If you play with your dog, you've probably heard it. And if you want your dog to play with you, panting at him is one of the best ways to get him to do it.

Do dogs pant like this simply because they are excited and breathless from playing hard? Maybe. But it is still

communication. It shows that the dog is having fun, and it changes the ways that the hearers behave. The sound of happy social panting, of dog laughter, can make other dogs happy, or at least calmer. When dogs at a shelter heard a recording of dog laughter, they barked and paced less and showed fewer signs of stress.

If panting can be laughter, barking is a shout. The loudness of sounds is measured in decibels, and two people talking calmly (like those walkers in the park) are probably speaking at about sixty decibels. Dog barks start at about seventy decibels and can reach up to a hundred and thirty. That is right up there with thunderclaps and planes taking off.

I can remember the first time a bark came out of Pump, when she was maybe three years old. She'd been so quiet until then, and then one day, after spending time with her barky German shepherd friend, a bark popped out of her. It was bark*like* more than a real bark, a *rurph!* that went along with a little leap off her front legs and a madly wagging tail. She got better at barking over the years, but it always felt like a new dog thing she was trying on.

It is too bad that barks are so loud, since that means that most human beings aren't fond of them. Barks are full of information that we might miss if we are wincing and covering our ears.

Wolves don't bark much. They may make an alarm bark, a sort of loud *woof!*, but this happens rarely, and it doesn't sound like the common dog barking you know from listening to your dog. Dogs, on the other hand, bark a lot. This makes some researchers think that barking is a system—even a language—that dogs developed so that they could communicate with humans.

There are other researchers who think that barking isn't really communicating much of anything. Sometimes dogs bark without an obvious reason, or without anyone around to hear. Sometimes they continue to bark long after you'd think any message would have been delivered. Think of a

ALEXANDRA HOROWITZ

dog barking over and over right in front of another dog. If there is a meaning in that bark, wouldn't once have been enough to make the second dog understand?

But moments like this may simply mean that this particular human researcher does not understand what the dog is trying to communicate. Or they may mean that this particular dog is not a good communicator. It's hard to be sure. But most researchers think that barks do have meaning. That meaning changes, however, depending on who is barking and what's going on when the barks are happening.

Dogs bark to get attention, to warn of danger, in fear, as a greeting, in play, or even out of loneliness, anxiety, confusion, distress, or pain. But they don't use the same bark for every situation. When researchers look at barks more closely, they can see that they are a mixture of the tones used in growls, whimpers, and yelps. Changing the mixture of these tones changes the kind of bark you get.

Researchers recorded dogs barking in three situations: a stranger ringing the doorbell, being locked outside, or playing. They found three clearly different kinds of barks. *Stranger barks* were the lowest in pitch and the harshest. They are well designed to send a message over a distance, and they can be combined into "superbarks," a series of loud, quick barks that most human listeners would call aggressive.

The *isolation bark* from a dog left outside tends to be higher in pitch. Some ranged from loud to soft and back again; some went from high-pitched to low. These barks are sent out one by one, with long pauses in between. People listening to them call them "fearful."

Play barks are also high in pitch, but they happen more quickly, one after the other. Unlike an isolation bark, they're aimed at someone in particular: another dog or a human playmate.

These differences between barks make sense. Remember that lower sounds tend to come from larger animals, and so a dog in a threatening situation (such as one worried about a stranger at the door) uses a lower tone in order to seem bigger. Higher sounds—whimpers, whines—are made by dogs hoping for attention or companionship. These are not warnings; they are requests. The dog making a play bark doesn't want to seem threatening, and so uses a higher-pitched sound.

These are not the only three situations in which dogs bark, of course. Each dog's bark sounds unique, and so dogs may simply bark to let others know where and who they are. Barks may show which group a dog belongs to, or they may help to bring a group together. Barking can be contagious, just like howling. One dog who barks may start off a chorus of barking dogs, all joined together in their shared noisiness.

Of course, not every sound a dog makes is a bark, a growl, or a whine. A dog can make noises with feet, teeth, or nose as well. A *play slap* is the sound of a dog jumping up and landing with both front feet on the ground at once.

It happens nearly every time dogs are playing together, and it can be a way a dog asks another dog (or a person) to play with him. Some dogs *chatter* their teeth when they are anxious and excited, so the clicking of teeth can warn that a dog is nervous or wary. And dogs *snuffle* when their heads are stretched high up and they are sniffing eagerly for food—and the snuffle can come to be a way dogs ask for food.

Dogs may not make the same noises we do—"Hello," "How are you?" "Get off my foot!" But they do communicate with sound. If we pay attention, they are saying a lot.

BODY AND TAIL

If Pump recognized someone approaching her on the street, her head would lower ever so slightly, and she would wag her tail low. This was quite different from her approach to a dog she was smitten with: tail high, head up, steady wagging. A dog she was already friends with would mean a different posture again: a looser, janglier approach, even an open-mouthed grab at the face, or a gentle bump with her hip along the other dog's body.

Sounds are useful signals, but dogs aren't limited to making noise if they want to communicate. They can use their bodies to send signals without making a sound.

Maybe you're sitting down right now, folded into a comfy chair. Or perhaps you're sprawled out on your bed. Most likely you don't *mean* anything by what you're doing with your body—it's just how you happened to settle down to read.

But at other times our posture means a great deal. A catcher crouches: He's prepared for a pitch. A parent crouches and opens his arms: He's inviting a child for a hug. Suppose you are outside and you see someone you know coming close. You might run up to say hello, or you might turn and run away. In each case, there is a body doing the same things—crouching or running. But in each case, the meaning is entirely different.

For animals who cannot make as many sounds with the mouth as humans can, posture becomes even more important. There is a language of the body, and for dogs its syllables are the rump, head, ears, legs, and tail.

Dogs understand this language easily. I learned it after watching hundreds of hours of dogs interacting with one another. We must look so boring to dogs! They can express everything from playfulness to aggression to adoration by changing the shapes of their bodies. Humans simply plod along, straight-backed, and we spend a lot of time either sitting still or traveling in a straight line. How dull.

When a dog simply stands at full height, with head and ears up, he is announcing that he is ready for anything. Even the hair along the shoulders or at the rump—what are called hackles—may be standing up, telling the world that the dog is alert and not about to back down. To make an even stronger statement, the dog might stand not just taller than another dog, but actually *over* that dog, putting his head or paws up on the other dog's back. That's about as clear a statement as you can make that you feel like you're in charge.

The opposite posture—crouching with head down, ears down, and tail tucked away—is conciliatory—a gesture of good will toward the other dog. To lie all the way down and show the belly is even more so.

The dog also uses his face, and particularly the mouth and ears, to send messages. A dog can "grin" with his mouth closed; this is a look of submission. The farther the mouth opens, the more the dog is showing excitement or stress. If his teeth are showing, the dog may be giving a warning. A dog may also yawn, opening his mouth wide with the teeth mostly covered. This isn't boredom (which is what a human yawn might indicate); it shows that the dog is anxious, timid, or stressed, and yawning seems to calm the dog and those nearby.

A dog's ears are also expressive. Standing tall, ears show that the dog is alert. Ears can also be relaxed or folded down tightly against the head, showing anxiety or fear. Eyes get in on the act too. Eyeballing another dog directly can be threatening or aggressive. To look away is submissive, calming the first dog's excitement and the second dog's anxiety.

As a puppy, her tail was trim, an arrow of soft black fur. This didn't last. It grew into an incredible banner of a tail, with long feathery hairs, and bent at the tip from an encounter with a car door when she was young. She waved it when excited or delighted. When lying down, she drummed it happily on the floor at my approach. If she was exhausted, her tail hung low and straight. She showed her lack of interest in a nosy dog by tucking her tail between her legs. Most of the time as we walked together, it hung loosely down and swished merrily to and fro. I loved to approach her slowly, stalking her, and prompt her tail to quiver into wagging.

ALEXANDRA HOROWITZ

There is a language of tails as well. One of the difficulties in translating it is that there are so many *kinds* of tails. There is the luxurious feathering of the golden retriever; then there's the tight corkscrew of the pug. Dogs wear tails long and rigid, stumpy and curled, hanging heavily, or always perky.

The wolf tail can be thought of as an "average" tail—long, slightly feathered, held naturally a bit down. Researchers have identified at least thirteen ways a wolf carries his tail, carrying thirteen different messages.

Dog tails held high show confidence, self-assertion, or excitement. That excitement can mean anything from cheerful interest to aggression. A tail high in the air also exposes the dog's rump, letting all the world smell who and what he is. Low-hanging tails, on the other hand, may show depression, stress, or anxiety. A long tail held so low as to curl between the legs closes off the rump to others, showing a dog who is submissive and fearful. When a dog is simply waiting around, his tail is relaxed, hanging low, dropped but not rigid. And a tail gently lifted, but not held up high, is a sign of mild interest or alertness.

But it is not as simple as tail height, for the tail is not just held—it is wagged. A wagging tail does not always mean a happy dog. Things are more complicated than that. How quickly and how hard the tail is wagged can tell you roughly how strongly your dog feels about what is going on.

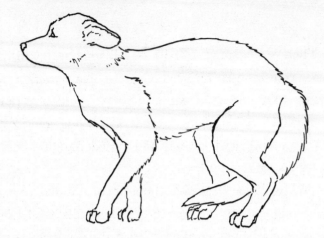

A high, stiffly wagging tail can be a threat, especially if it comes attached to a dog holding himself straight and tall. A quick wag of a low, drooping tail (like the one attached to a dog who has just eaten your best shoes) is a sign of submission. A tail wagging lightly comes with a dog who is interested but not quite sure yet. A loose, lively, whisking tail comes with a search for a ball lost in high grass or pursuing a fascinating smell on the ground. And the happy wag is incredibly different from all of these. This is the wag you probably see when you come home from school—the tail is held above or out from the body and draws rough, strong arcs in the air behind it. It means unmistakable delight.

Even a tail that is *not* wagging can tell you something. Dogs tend to hold their tails still when they are paying careful attention to something—maybe a ball in your hand or maybe your face as they wait for you to tell them what is about to happen next.

ALEXANDRA HOROWITZ

There is more detail to the tail wag than you have probably ever guessed. Dogs tend to wag more to their right side when they suddenly see their owners or something else they are interested in—maybe another person or a cat. When they catch sight of an unfamiliar dog, they still wag, but more to the left. You may not be able to see this with your own dog unless you watch a slow-motion video of his tail in action, but consider yourself lucky to be wagged at with such enthusiasm.

Dogs may be saying a lot with their madly wagging tails or flattened ears. But there is an even more important way they communicate with each other. Neither sound nor sight is a match for smell when it comes to passing on information. Dogs have a very smelly thing handy most of the time—their own urine.

When a dog lets loose a stream of urine, it may not look much like two people having a chat. But it some ways it is.

When people communicate, we make careful choices about whom we are talking with. We don't yammer out loud to our own left hands. Instead, we find someone who can understand what we're saying, who's near enough to hear us, and who's not too distracted to listen. Then we tell that person something. This is one of the ways we can tell that someone is communicating, and not just making noise. It's called communicating with intention, by deliberate choice.

Urine marking is peeing with intention. It isn't done just for the sake of emptying the bladder. Dogs do this too, of course, but when they are marking, they squeeze just a little urine out of their bladders at a time. This allows them to spread a scent far and wide as they travel. For males (and some females, too), urine marking goes along with a raised leg that seems to make the whole operation more obvious and helps the dog to aim, so that the urine goes right where he wants it.

Dogs make the same kind of careful choices about peeing that humans do when we decide whom to talk to and how to talk to them. Watch a dog sniff his way down the street; he will sniff more locations than he squirts. Dogs are very particular about where they leave their smells. Who has marked before them, the time of year, and who's nearby all affect how and where a dogs pees. This consideration turns peeing into a kind of conversation.

What kind of conversation? What messages are being sent? We know that each dog's smell is unique, so that by leaving small deposits of urine they must be saying something about who they are and where they've been. A dog's odor is his identity.

But dogs are saying more with their urine than simply "This is who I am and I was here." If we look at this behavior closely, we can figure out more.

It was once thought that these messages mark the dog's territory, leaving a sign to warn off other dogs. But new research shows that this is probably not the case. (We might have guessed it by the fact that dogs don't usually pee in the corners of their houses—their real "territory.") The invisible pile of scents on a hydrant is more like a community bulletin board than a NO TRESPASSERS sign. Old announcements, fading fast, peek out from under more recent notes. The ones who come by most often naturally end up at the top of the heap.

So if dogs aren't saying "this is mine, keep off," what *are* they saying when they pee? Our first hint is that puppies don't urine mark. So the conversation must have to do with something that only matters to adult dogs. We also know that dogs only urine mark when other dogs are around. Dogs who are kept penned by themselves urinate, of course (they have to), but they don't leave small amounts as a message, and males kept in a pen rarely lift a leg to mark.

So when dogs urine mark, they are sending messages on purpose, for other dogs, for adults only. Those messages are probably about mating. Dogs talk a lot—with their tails, with their ears, with their entire bodies—but conversations with their urine are most likely about who is looking for a mate and who is ready to find one.

WITHOUT WORDS

So do dogs use language? Not as we do. Do they communicate? Absolutely. They send messages to each other and they send them to us.

The very fact that dogs do not use language makes me treasure them more. Their silence can be very endearing.

Dogs are silent not because they cannot speak but because they do not need to. There is no awkwardness in a shared silent moment with a dog. Maybe a dog gazes quietly at me from the other side of the room; maybe he stretches out sleepily alongside me. There are no words here, but plenty of communication.

DOG-EYED

It takes all of six seconds for Pump to go from being masterful to being foolish. In the first five seconds she dodges between brambles and bushes and trees to catch a fast-moving tennis ball. It thonks off a tree and she's there to practically vacuum it into her mouth. Another dog tears in from nowhere and Pump hurtles away, dodging this stealer of tennis balls. Then it's the sixth second. She stops, suddenly confused. She's lost track of me. I'm within sight; I smile at her. She still doesn't see where I am. Instead, she spots a large, limping man with a heavy coat and takes off after him. I have to run to catch her.

If we human beings had to rank our senses from least to most important, sight would be the winner by a long shot. There's barely a challenge for second place, either—hearing is part of nearly every experience we have.

It's not that smell, touch, or taste don't matter to us.

But most of the time, if we notice something unusual or unexpected, we turn to examine it with our eyes. We don't learn about it by inhaling it closely or taking a bold lick.

This system of ranking the senses is turned upside-down for a dog. Snout beats eyes, time and time again. Now that we know how well dogs can smell, it makes sense that vision is less important to them. When a dog turns his head toward you, it is not so much to look at you with his eyes. Rather, it is to get his nose to look at you. The eyes just come along for the ride.

What do dogs even need their eyes for? They can find their way around and discover food with their remarkable noses. Anything that needs closer examination goes right in the mouth. They've got the vomeronasal organ for checking out other dogs. But as it turns out, they do need their eyes for at least two important things: to help out their other senses, and to look at us.

When we think about how dogs' eyes got to be the way they are, we can look again to wolves—and to one particular part of a wolf's life: eating.

Smell is important to wolves and their relatives, but it isn't the only signal that food may be nearby. A trail left on the ground may be easy for a nose to follow, but odors drifting on the breeze may waft away. Their source can be difficult to pinpoint. Prey that is running can move more quickly than the smell it leaves on the air. But even on a windy day, even if an animal is moving fast, a wolf can still see that it's there.

So once a wolf gets a quick sniff of something tasty nearby, it uses its eyes to locate the prey. Many prey animals are camouflaged to blend in with their surroundings. The camouflage only works, however, as long as the prey holds still. So wolves are very good at spotting movement. And since the wolf's prey is most active at dusk or dawn, wolves developed eyes that are especially sensitive in low light.

At first glance those prey-tracking eyes that dogs inherited from their wolflike ancestors look a fair bit like ours. But there are differences.

Take a look in a mirror and then at your dog's face, and you'll notice something about your eyes and his. Human eyes have a dark pupil surrounded by a lighter, colored iris. The pupil and iris are in turn surrounded by the white of the eye. This makes it very clear to other people where we are looking. The movement of our dark pupils and bright irises is very easy to see against the white that surrounds them.

Not so in most dogs. Dogs tend to have very little white to their eyes, and the pupil and iris together are often so dark they remind me of bottomless lakes. It is much easier to tell where your dog is looking by seeing where he turns his head, rather than by watching his eyes.

If you keep looking in that mirror, you'll find another difference. Your eyes are smack in the front of your face.

This means that humans can see anything right before us in high detail, great focus, and strong color. Objects that are to the sides fade away. This is very helpful for an animal (like us) who needs to be able to tell other humans apart. Your eyes let you know, quickly, whether that blob of color coming at you is your friend or your mortal enemy.

Dogs' eyes are not as good at seeing what is right in front of them. (If you've ever watched a dog search helplessly for a toy he is about to step on, this is why: Most dogs don't have the vision to see the toy clearly unless they take a step back.) Instead, most dogs see a wide, panoramic view of all that is around them. They can see much more of what's alongside their heads than a human being can. Dogs with long noses (think retrievers) have the best side-to-side vision; dogs with short noses (like pugs) have the worst. (These dogs, in fact, have vision a bit more like humans, with better focus right in front of them.)

Some of the differences between dog breeds can be explained by their vision. Dogs with excellent side-to-side vision (and long noses) are usually "ball dogs," who love to play fetch. Because their eyes spot movement well and can see from side to side of your lawn, retrievers can easily see a tennis ball traveling across the grass. A short-nosed shih tzu isn't known for fetching, partly because he just doesn't see the ball as easily. If the ball travels to the side of his head, he cannot spot it anymore; for him, it simply disappears. This is why a pug is likelier to sit on your lap and stare at your face adoringly than to retrieve a Frisbee, and a Labrador is more likely to fetch a ball than to sit on your lap (well, there are lots of good reasons for that!).

What about color? Many people believe that dogs are color-blind, but that is incorrect. It is true, however, that color plays a less important role for them than it does for humans. Dog eyes do not see color as strongly as yours do. Colors that are bright and vivid to you are probably duller and dimmer to your dog. And there are some colors we see that dogs can't.

Our eyes respond to the colors red, blue, or green. Everything we see comes in a combination of these three colors. Dogs' eyes pick up blue and greenish-yellow. They don't see red, or orange, or yellow the same way we do. An apple that looks bright red to you probably looks more like faint green to your dog.

To imagine what the world looks like to your dog, think about how you see colors at dusk, right before night. If you're outside when night falls, take a look around you. In this low light, colors are not as vivid to your eyes. You might notice the bright green of the leaves growing slowly duller. You can still see the ground underfoot, but the details—the edges of grass blades, the scattering of flower petals—are lost.

You can still *see*, of course. Your eyes notice color at dusk. You can still detect lights and darks. But the richness of color has faded. Details are less sharp. This may be how your dog sees, even in the brightest daylight.

If humans are better at noticing color, dogs have a different advantage: Their eyes can gather more light. Their eyes are sensitive to even very small amounts of light. Also, once light travels through a dog's eye, it strikes a triangle of tissue behind the eyeball. Other animals, including cats, have this bit of tissue, but not humans. It reflects the light back through the animal's eye a second time. This means that the dog's eyes receive twice the light that yours do. (It also accounts for all those photographs you have of your dog with brilliant light shining out where his eyes should be. This is the light of your camera's flash reflecting off the tissue inside the dog's eye.)

So dogs see quite well just when our eyes start to work *less* well: at dusk and at night. The same parts of the dog's eye that pick up low light so well are also the parts of the eye that help the dog see motion. If your dog can't seem to find his ball, you can make it magically "appear" to his eyes by giving it a little shove.

Wolves are especially good at catching prey because they have eyes that work well in low light and are excellent at spotting motion. Unlike his long-ago wolflike ancestors, your dog isn't likely to have to pull down a caribou for lunch. But he might want to catch a Frisbee that you throw to him. And there is one more detail about the structure of the dog's eye that makes Frisbee-catching, among other things, easier.

When light reaches the eye of a dog or a human—in

fact, of any mammal—it must be translated into electrical signals that are then carried to the brain. The brain then translates the electrical signals into an image—and that's when we feel that we've "seen" something. Say, a Frisbee whizzing through the air.

Because of the way the cells in our eyes work, we don't actually see the motion of the ball. What our brains receive is a sequence of still pictures, one after the other. We see so many of these pictures so quickly—sixty every second—that we *think* we're seeing a moving ball. Our brains make the snapshots into a movie.

Dogs' brains receive more "pictures" from their eyes than human brains do—about seventy or eighty per second. This doesn't mean that the world moves faster to a dog. What it means is that they see a bit *more* world in every second than we do. It's easier for a dog to catch a Frisbee in midair than it is for us because the dog can see it falling just a fraction of a second before we can. Then the dog can move into the right position to grab it.

We must always seem a little slow to dogs. Our responses to the Frisbee, and to the world, are just a split second behind theirs.

THE WORLD A DOG SEES

As she gets older, Pump suddenly doesn't want to enter the elevator when we come inside after a walk. Perhaps she doesn't see its dark insides as well after the bright light outside. I encourage her, or jump in myself first, or throw something light-colored on the elevator floor for her to see. Finally, every time, she musters up her courage and leaps in, as though jumping across an enormous pit. Brave girl.

So dogs can see some of the same things we see, but they don't see them in the same way. Knowing more about how a dog's eyes are structured can help us understand a lot of the ways dogs behave.

When you are watching your dog, remember that he sees what is on either side of him well, but what is right in front of him less well. His own paws are probably not in terrific focus to him. Dogs don't use their paws much in dealing with their world, at least not when compared to how much people use their hands. The fact that they can't see them well has something to do with this (along with the fact that, of course, they do not have fingers or thumbs). A small difference in vision leads to far less reaching, grabbing, and handling.

In the same way, dogs can bring our faces into focus, but can't detect our eyes as well. This means your dog will catch the expression on your face, but not a meaningful glare. If you point or turn toward something, a dog will look at it, but he won't follow a quick glance out of the corner of your eye.

Dogs use their vision to help out their other senses. First, a dog might hear a noise, but only have a rough idea where that noise is coming from. So he will turn his head that way, allowing him to use his eyes to pinpoint the source of the interesting sound . . . which he can then examine closely by nose.

Living in a world of smells, with eyes that are different than ours, dogs do not see the world exactly as we do. And sometimes they see details that we cannot.

Humans see so much that we learn to block out details. We take one broad look when we enter a room, and then, if everything is more or less where we expect it to be, we stop looking. As you are walking along a familiar route to school, you are not checking out each tree, each house, each blade of grass. You pay attention to the landmarks (turn left by the red house; cross the street at the light) and nothing more.

There is good reason to believe that this is not how dogs see the world. When we walk our dogs to the park day after day, the way becomes familiar to us over time. But dogs don't stop looking. They are much more struck by what they actually see (or smell)—the details right in front of them—than by what they expect to see.

Now that we know how dogs see, a new question comes up. What do dogs look at? Since they are clever animals, they look at us. Once a dog has opened up his eyes to us, a remarkable thing happens. He starts gazing at people, perhaps even seeing things about us that we do not see ourselves. Soon it seems that dogs are looking straight into our minds.

SEEN BY A DOG

I am startled and a little flustered to look up from my work and see Pump watching me. There is a powerful pull to a dog who looks you in the eyes. I am on her radar. It feels that she is looking not just at me, but to—and into—me.

Look a dog in the eyes, and you get the definite feeling that he is looking back. Dogs return our gaze. They aren't just noticing that we are there; they are looking at us in the same way that we look at them.

When someone looks at us the way a dog does, it suggests something about their mind. A gazer is *paying attention* to you, and, possibly, paying attention to whether you are paying attention back.

Attention means more than just seeing or hearing. Any animal with eyes and ears can see or hear, but *attention* is singling out one particular thing and bringing it to the forefront of the mind. It is *considering* what you are looking at or listening to.

At its simplest, attention is simply the ability to focus on some things while ignoring others. This is vital for any animal. It can mean survival. Out of all of the objects an animal sees, smells, or hears, some are food, some are threats, and some are simply there. If an animal learns to focus on the parts of its surroundings that will either kill it or help it survive, that animal has a better chance of reaching a comfortable old age.

Most people today do not have to worry about being eaten by a predator. We don't have to forage for food in the wilderness. But we still need to direct our attention. Over and over, we have to pull our attention away from what does not matter right now and apply it to what does. We need attention to get through the simplest tasks of our day: listen to someone talking to us, plan how to get to school, remember what we were thinking about a moment ago.

Dogs are something like us in this way. Most of their survival needs are taken care of. They live in warm houses and have food delivered in bowls. But they still need to figure out how to pay attention to what matters. What makes dogs stand out from other animals, even other domesticated creatures, is the way that they pay attention to *us*. To people. They are alert to where we are, to our movements, to our moods, and most importantly, to our faces.

As human beings, we pay a lot of attention to other human beings because doing so helps us predict what they will do next, or what they can see, or what they might know. This tendency to watch others, to think about others, to figure out what others know or might do, is part of what makes us human.

So why do dogs look at us so much? When they do it, what do they understand about us? These questions have been the subject of much new research. The way that people learn to pay attention as they grow from babies to adults has been well studied. Lately, scientists have been studying dogs to see if they learn to pay attention to others in the same ways that human children do.

THE ATTENTION OF ANIMALS

Pump comes within an inch of me and starts
panting at me, eyes wide and unblinking. She
is telling me that she needs something.

After they open their eyes, do animals look at things on purpose? Do they gaze at things carefully, choosing what to look at? Do they notice others' eyes? Do they understand what it means to pay attention to someone else, and what it means if that someone is paying attention back? These are some of the questions that researchers are trying to answer.

Researchers who are studying this ask themselves what animals understand about what other living things might be thinking. Does a cat think of a mouse as an animal with a life and a mind of its own, or just as a moving meal that must be quickly caught and eaten? When a caged chimpanzee looks at a human zookeeper, is he considering anything about that zookeeper? Does he wonder how to get her to open the door? Does he wonder anything at all? Or is he simply waiting to see what this colorful, moving object nearby him will do?

It's a tricky question to answer. No animal has told us in words what its life is like, or picked up a pencil and paper to write it down. The only real way for animals to tell us what is going on inside them is with their behavior.

But there are pitfalls here. It's hard to be sure if one animal's behavior means the same thing as another's. For instance, I smile when I am happy. Maybe you're smiling because you're happy too. Or maybe you're nervous. Or surprised. Or even concerned. The smile is a clue that something is going on inside both of us . . . but it doesn't tell us exactly what that something is.

Still, behavior is the best clue we have about what is happening inside an animal's mind. We'll look at three things dogs do and see what these behaviors tell us about attention.

Dogs Gaze

First, there is gaze—the act of looking carefully and intently at something. It is definitely something that dogs do. Looking at something seems simple, but it means more than you might think. Gaze is a hint that attention is being paid. And attention is a big deal, both to whoever is doing the gazing and the person who is being gazed at.

Looking hard at another person is almost like *doing* something to that person. Try it and see. Take a careful look at someone nearby. Don't shift your gaze away (even if it starts to feel uncomfortable—and it likely will). How long before that person looks up to ask you what on earth you're doing?

Eye contact is important to animals too. Between apes, eye contact can be aggressive. Submissive animals will avoid it. To stare at a dominant animal is to invite an attack from that animal. Submissive chimpanzees look down at the ground or at their own feet, only taking quick glances around. They are trying to avoid staring at anyone *and* being stared at themselves.

Wolves are similar. One wolf staring directly at another can be taken as a threat. So we'd expect dogs to do as wolves and chimpanzees and many other animals do—carefully avoid eye contact, in case they threaten a larger, stronger animal without meaning to.

But dogs do not do this. Dogs look at our faces. They look at each other as well. So something has changed with dogs. They must get something useful, something important, out of eye contact. Whatever they get, it is important enough to overcome the ancient fear passed on by their ancestors that looking at anyone too hard is risky.

That ancient fear still exists. If another dog who seems

aggressive or too interested comes near, your dog may look to one side, trying to calm things down. And if you stare unblinkingly at your dog, he'll probably look away. But the fact that dogs *will* look us in the eyes (even if not all the time) is important. It shows that gaze matters in some way to them.

And dogs don't just look at us. They look wherever we look.

Dogs Follow a Gaze

It doesn't happen at once. But not long after bringing a dog or a puppy to your home for the first time, you might notice something. Nothing in your house is safe.

Dogs train humans to become suddenly tidy. You find yourself putting away shoes and socks right when you take them off, taking out the trash before it gets to the top of the container, and leaving nothing on the floor that could fit in the mouth of a puppy with new teeth and lots of curiosity.

So you start putting everything away behind closed doors, into shut cabinets, onto high shelves. Your dog is baffled. The shoe, hat, or takeout container he wanted so much has suddenly disappeared. But soon you will notice that your dog has learned something new. *You* are the one making things vanish, and you usually give your secrets away.

How? You look.

When you pick up a sock and set it down, it isn't just your hand involved. You need your eyes as well. You look where you are going—or where the sock is going. Later, you may tell your dog to leave your socks alone and, at the same time, glance toward where you left that sock you picked up. Your dog's head turns to follow your gaze.

Gaze following—looking where someone else is looking. Human infants learn to do it before they are one year old. Dogs do it even sooner.

You can think of gaze as a way of pointing without using your hands. And we know that dogs can follow a pointing finger. Researchers have tested this ability. In one experiment, a biscuit or other tasty food is hidden under one of two turned-over buckets. After the researchers carefully make sure that the food cannot be smelled, a dog is brought into the room. He must choose one of two buckets. If he chooses the right one, the food is his. If not, no food for him.

A person who knows where the food is hidden is standing there to give the dog some help. The question is, will dogs understand the help? The answer is yes—most of the time. Dogs pick up a simple point of the finger, a point that reaches across the researcher's body, points from *behind* the body, and even points with elbows, knees, and legs. They will even follow a point from a life-size video image of their owner.

Most remarkable of all, dogs don't actually need a point

ALEXANDRA HOROWITZ

to pick up information about which bucket is hiding their treat. All the researcher has to do is turn his or her head and look at the bucket. A dog can follow the researcher's gaze.

In this experiment, dogs followed a point or a gaze about 70 to 85 percent of the time. That's even better than chimpanzees, which is remarkable. Chimps, after all, have arms and fingers, the basic equipment necessary to point at things. You'd think a chimp would understand pointing even better than a dog. But it's dogs who show a clearer understanding of pointing, and dogs who get that a gaze can be a kind of point.

A dog performs worse, though, than a three-year-old human. (A three-year-old child *always* understands what a pointing finger means.) So dogs don't understand a point quite as well, or in quite the same way, as a very young person. But they *do* seem to understand it. A pointing finger or a pointed gaze is a way of saying without words, "Direct your attention there—something good is waiting." Dogs get it.

And dogs get something even more complicated about attention. They don't just direct their attention where we want them to. They can also tell us where to direct *our* attention.

Attention-Getting

How does your dog tell you he needs to go outside? That he wants you to throw a ball for him? Or where a tasty treat fell behind the couch when you were out of the room? Experiments and studies of dogs at play show that dogs seem to understand how to get our attention and how to use that attention to ask for what they want. They also seem to understand when we are *not* paying attention (so that they can get away with something forbidden).

"Attention-getting" behavior—you're familiar with it. You probably know it as anything that your dog does to interfere with what you are trying to do. Do you want to tie your shoelaces, eat a meal, read this book? Your dog would prefer you to scratch his ears, give him a bite to eat, or take him for a walk. How can he get you to cooperate?

By changing the place where you have put your attention.

There are methods of doing this—getting in the way of your gaze, making a noise, touching. Your dog may jump on you, or bark, or just put his face close to yours so that you have no choice but to look at him. Guide dogs for blind owners sometimes slurp loudly enough for their owners to hear in order to get their attention.

Dogs work to get the attention of other dogs as well, particularly when they are looking for someone to play with. A dog might "mirror" the behavior of another dog, maybe coming to drink from the same bowl (and taking the opportunity to lick his face). Or if one dog has a stick in his mouth, a second dog may grab a stick of his own.

ALEXANDRA HOROWITZ

Some dogs try the same behavior over and over. One might stand over a tennis ball, barking and barking, while his owner chats with another human. The bark is a good attention-getter, but not if it fails to get the human to throw the ball. This dog would be better off trying something else.

Other dogs seem to understand that if one kind of attention-getter fails, it's best to try another. Suppose you are curled up in a chair with this book. Your dog comes close. You don't look up. He wanders off, only to return with a shoe or something else he's not supposed to have in his mouth. Probably this makes you scold him, remove the shoe, and return to your book. More serious tactics are needed. Next he may whine or let out a soft woof. Then he moves on to contact: a slight push with a wet nose, nuzzling, or jumping. Maybe he even drops to the floor at your feet with a loud sigh. He is doing his best with you here.

So far, dogs can do all the things a young child learns to do—gazing, following a point, following a gaze, and using attention-getters. Do they also point, as best as they can, with their bodies? Do they point with their heads to direct our attention to a particular place? To show us something?

Researchers came up with a way to find out. In one study, a dog watches an experimenter hide a treat—out of the dog's reach. Then the dog's owner walked into the room. Would the dog see the owner as a tool for getting the treat? And how would he tell the person what he needed to do?

In these experiments, it seemed that the humans were the only animals in the room who were slow to get what was going on. The dogs first used attention-getting behavior (such as barking) to be sure their human noticed them. Then, most importantly, they used their gazes. They looked back and forth between the owner and the location of the hidden treat.

They showed their owners where the treat was hidden. In other words, they pointed with their eyes.

You may have seen this same behavior in your own home, although you may not have realized what your dog was doing. If your dog loves to fetch, he probably brings his balls back and drops them at your feet. But always in *front* of you, never behind. He drops his ball where you will be sure to notice it (and hopefully you'll get the clue and throw it again).

If the ball does end up behind you for some reason, the dog has a bunch of attention-getters to use, followed by relentless looking from your face to the ball. You; ball. You; ball. Finally you'll get the hint, turn around, pick up the ball, and throw it. You'll follow your dog's pointing eyes and put your attention right where he wants it to be.

There is one more thing dogs do with human attention. They figure out how to use that attention to get the things they want. And even more remarkably, they use human attention to get away with forbidden things they want to do.

Dogs Use Attention to Their Advantage
Researchers asked another question about dogs and attention. Can dogs use the attention of people to figure

out how to get something for themselves?

It seems that they can.

In one experiment, dogs were presented with a person holding a sandwich—a natural opportunity for the dog to beg for a bite. But when the sandwich-holder was either blindfolded or facing away from the dog, the dog did not bother to beg. If there was a non-blindfolded person handy, the dog begged that person instead.

What does this tell us? First, if your dog is begging at the table, it's probably because you've made eye contact (even just long enough to say "No begging!"). You've shown the dog, with your eyes, that your attention is available. Second, a dog knows that a human who can't see him isn't likely to hand out bites of her sandwich. The human's gaze is not on the dog—therefore the human's attention is not there. And it'll be more useful to go and beg from someone else.

Dogs have patiently gone through this experiment, dealing with humans who are blindfolded, wearing buckets over their heads, or holding books up in front of their eyes. Again and again, the dogs show that, more often than not, they will beg from the person whose eyes they can see. (Human beings act the same way. We prefer to talk to, beg, or ask favors from people whose eyes we can see.) Eyes equal attention, attention equals knowledge. People come to understand this very early in life. Dogs seem to understand it too.

They can also understand what it means when attention is taken away.

In one experiment, researchers watched to see how dogs reacted to the command *lie down*. It turned out that the dogs' behavior changed according to how much attention their owners paid after making the request.

If an owner said, "Lie down!" and stood there staring at the dog, the dog stayed down. Perfectly obedient.

If an owner said, "Lie down!" and then turned his gaze to the TV, the dog lay still for a little while, but shortly got up again.

If an owner said, "Lie down!" and left the room, the dogs were quickest to disobey.

This may not seem surprising to you if you own a dog. You've probably seen your dog do similar things. Maybe you know that your dog won't jump up on the counter to get your lunch if you're in the kitchen. But if you go into the living room for a second, all bets are off.

Now think for a moment about what this means. Your dog notices how much attention his owner is paying. Then your dog changes his behavior along with that attention.

This is something that two-year-old humans, chimps, monkeys, and dogs do. There are *no other animals* (that we know of, anyway) who can understand attention in this way.

If you are thinking that you might use this information to trick your dog into behaving himself while you are at school by simply pretending to be around, maybe by video or over speakerphone, I have bad news for you. When experimenters tried showing dogs a life-size video image of their owners, dogs did not seem inclined to behave themselves. Instead, they carried on exactly as they did when their owners were not home. If the videotaped owners pointed to some hidden food, the dogs could follow those hints. But they did not obey commands from videos of their owners.

If you want your dog to follow your every command, you'd better plan on staying right beside him and keeping your attention on him. He can tell if you don't.

DOGS WHO STUDY HUMANS

A dog who gazes at us is seeing us. Is he also thinking about us, the same way we might be thinking about the dog? What does the dog know about human beings?

We are known by our dogs—probably far better than we know them. They are eavesdroppers and Peeping Toms. They quietly spy on our every move. They know our comings and goings and our habits, and they're aware of how long we spend in the bathroom or in front of the television. They know what we eat and what we eat too much of. They watch us like no other animal watches us.

We share our homes with uncounted numbers of mice, millipedes, and mites. None bothers to look our way. We open our door and see pigeons, squirrels, and assorted flying bugs; they barely notice us. But our dogs watch us. They watch us from across the room, from the window, and out of the corners of their eyes. They watch to see what we will do, and they watch to see what we are watching. They watch to see where our attention goes.

Dogs study us as if they are scientists and we are their

research projects. Small children do the same thing. They stare at the adults around them, watching their moods, their words, their actions. They gaze with equal fascination at a man limping down the street or a swirl of leaves caught up in a whirlwind. As human beings grow older, we stop paying so much attention. Once we learn the basics—the wind blows leaves around; people cry when sad, shout when angry, and smile when happy—we don't need to study our world so closely. So we don't. We fall out of the habit of paying close attention.

Dogs don't. They notice the limping man, the leaves tumbling down the sidewalk, human faces. All of these get long looks from the dogs who pass them. What makes dogs such good scientists of human behavior is that they naturally pay attention to us. They notice what is normal behavior and what is different. They never stop looking.

CAN DOGS READ MINDS?

Sometimes dogs can be so sensitive to their humans that it seems magical. Dogs know not just what we're doing, but what we're about to do. They seem to know us inside and out. Can they read minds?

Not exactly. But they can read us.

Dogs pay attention to us. And they use their senses—their eyes, their ears, their marvelously sensitive noses—to investigate us. They discover a lot.

Our dogs know how we look, and even more, how

ALEXANDRA HOROWITZ

we smell. They also know how we act. I can recognize Pumpernickel not just by her face, but also by her walk—a jaunty trot, just a bit off-kilter, her droopy ears bouncing in step. Dogs know us the same way. How we move and what we do is a part of who we are.

Say you are simply walking across a room. That act, all by itself, is full of information for the dog watching you. Are you walking across the room to get a book that you left on the couch? Your dog probably stays put. Are you getting ready to take him for a walk? You have a bouncing, panting, delighted companion at your side.

How did he know?

Of course, sometimes you give off obvious clues. Maybe you put on your shoes, grabbed a leash or a jacket, or said *that word* (instead of carefully spelling W-A-L-K). Then it would be reasonable that your dog knew a walk was in store. But what if you did none of that? What if all you did was look up from your homework or get up from your chair, and your dog was still on to you?

If you looked up quickly, with a movement that says, "I'm done! Time to go!," or if you got up to walk briskly across the room, that's all an attentive dog needs to figure out what you're up to. Your dog has spent a lot of time watching you. He knows what you're doing before you're even aware that you're giving him hints.

As we've seen, dogs are sensitive to where you're looking and what you're looking at. You hold your head one way when you're looking down at your math homework. You hold it another way when you're looking over at the front door. The difference is very clear to your dog. Even small movements—what you're doing with your hands or how you're sitting in your chair—are noticeable to a dog.

Bigger movements are as obvious as someone shouting. If you spend three hours motionless in front of a computer, and then suddenly stand and stretch your arms overhead—you've been transformed in the eyes of your dog. The fact that your attention has shifted away from the computer is crystal clear. A hopeful dog can easily decide that the change means you're finally ready to go get the leash.

Dogs can tell what we are about to do partly because of how their bodies are built, and partly because of how their minds work. We know that dogs' eyes are excellent at seeing motion—this gives them a bit of a head start when it comes to noticing you close your math book or shift in your chair. They can react to your movements a fraction of a second before you know there is anything to react to. Since they pay such good attention to us, dogs notice useful connections between one thing happening and another happening. A human gets a can out of a cupboard, and food follows. A human stirs from a chair and looks toward the door, and it's time for a walk.

Many owners claim that their dogs can do more than tell when they're ready for a walk or when food is on its way. Their dogs can read character, they say. They know who is to be trusted and who isn't. They can pick out a person who will be a good friend. Can dogs really do this?

To answer this question, we have to think about two things. First, about the owners. An owner might remember how her dog once growled at someone she didn't trust. But does the owner remember all the times the dog stayed quiet when someone untrustworthy was about? Probably not.

Second, about the dogs: A dog can tell how *you* feel about that person. If you feel nervous or anxious about an approaching stranger, you show it, however much you're trying to hide your feelings. Your dog can tell. Dogs can smell changes that stress causes in your body. They can also notice tense muscles and quick breathing. So a dog might not be telling you that *he* knows that a new person is untrustworthy; he might be telling you that *you* don't trust that person.

Or the dog might actually notice some things about that approaching stranger. Someone who is not trustworthy—who is trying to deceive you—may not look you in the eye. His glance may dart here and there. Dogs notice this gaze. Someone who is aggressive may stare angrily, move too slowly or too quickly, or turn aside from a straight path to move toward you. Dogs notice this behavior.

In one experiment, researchers tested this ability by seeing how dogs responded to strangers. They asked different people, unknown to the dog, to approach him. Some were

told to behave in a friendly way—walking at a normal speed, talking to the dog in a cheerful voice, gently petting the dog. Others were asked to behave in an unfriendly way—walking toward the dog at an unpredictable pace, without talking, and staring at the dog.

It's not surprising, really, that dogs reacted differently to different kinds of strangers. They greeted the friendly ones and avoided the unfriendly ones. The dogs read the humans' behavior and changed their own behavior according to what they saw and heard.

But there is one other bit of information this experiment offers. When the people in the experiment were asked to *switch* their behavior—when a formerly friendly person suddenly acted threatening—how did the dogs respond? Not all the same way. Some dogs acted as if the person with the new behavior was an entirely new person, an unfriendly one. Some did not. They knew the person by her smell, and the new behavior, although odd, did not change her into someone new. The ways dogs recognized a person was a combination of her behavior—what they could see or hear—and her smell.

> One winter we took a trip north and were treated to a large snowstorm. We pulled out sleds, found a great big hill, and skidded down it. Pump reacted in a new way. She ferociously chased us on each ride down, biting, grabbing, and growling at our faces. I couldn't stop her for all of my laughing. Pump was playing, but it was a play I had not seen before, a play with real aggression in it. When I got to the bottom of the hill and managed to stand up and shake off my covering of snow, she calmed down at once.

So dogs are careful, clever watchers, but they are not magicians or mind readers. And it *is* possible to fool them. Pump was fooled when I leapt on that sled. For all of her keen senses, she did not recognize that I was still me. As far as she could tell, I had changed. I was lying down, I was covered in winter clothing, I was dusted with snow. Most importantly, I was moving entirely differently. Instead of an upright companion, slowly walking at her side, I was more like a smoothly moving, high-speed prey animal.

Others dogs react the same way to people on bicycles, skateboards, in-line skates, even people out for a run. The person on the bike or skates is suddenly moving very differently. They roll! Quickly! This changes them in the dog's eyes. Instead of a familiar person, they become something to chase.

If you want to stop a dog from chasing a bicycle, the answer is simple—stop the bike. The chasing impulse triggered by the dog's sensitive eyes will stop when the unusual motion stops.

ALL ABOUT YOU

Even though dogs can sometimes be fooled, they know us well. Their attention is powerful. Their senses are keen. It's remarkable what a dog's careful attention and powerful senses let that dog discover about the people in his life.

Being known by our dog and even having our dog predict our actions is part of why we are so fond of them. Dogs study and learn about us. They watch how we act with other people. They keep their eyes on our attention, our focus, our gaze. They can't read our minds, but they know us. They can tell what we are about to do.

THE MIND OF A DOG

It's dawn and I try to sneak out of the room without waking Pump, tip-toeing and holding my breath. I can't see her dark eyes, camouflaged against her black fur. Her head rests peacefully between her legs. At the door I think I've made it. But then I see her lifted eyebrows tracking my path. She's on to me.

The dog, as we've seen, is a master looker. Is there a thinking, plotting mind behind that look? We know that dogs are skilled at understanding and even using attention. What does this mean about the dog's brain? What are dogs thinking about? Do they think about other dogs? About themselves? About you? Are dogs *smart*?

DOG SMARTS

Dog owners sometimes share stories about how smart their dogs are. "My dog knew I was coming home before I even got there!" they might say. Or "Look, he's trying to fool me!" or "He always knows when he's done something wrong." News reports even announce that dogs are smart enough to use words, count, or call 911 in an emergency.

Are these things that owners say about their dogs actually true? Can we believe these news stories? And if all of these stories *are* true, what does that tell us about the way that dogs think?

Scientists have a name for the stories told by owners and sometimes reported by the news—anecdotes. An anecdote might be a story about how one dog did something once that looked clever. But an anecdote, by itself, is not proof the dog was aware of what he was doing, or that all dogs can do that clever thing.

Instead, researchers design studies that test these kinds of anecdotes about what dogs think and know. Before researchers began studying dogs, other people sold "intelligence tests" for dogs! You may have taken an intelligence test for humans—pen-and-paper creations that test your vocabulary, math skills, pattern-finding, attention to detail. These kinds of questions might give us a rough idea of how smart a person is, but obviously IQ tests for humans won't work with dogs.

Instead of vocabulary words, dog IQ tests asked things like: How well does a dog obey commands? Can he remember where a treat is hidden? Learn a new trick? These tests loosely measured, in dogs, some of the same things we look for in humans—but were mostly for entertainment, not knowledge.

More recently, researchers have designed more sophisticated studies of the mind of dogs. They ask questions like, Can dogs, like human children, come to understand that something exists even if they cannot see or smell it? (If a treat is hidden under a cup, do dogs know that it is still there?) Can dogs learn? (Can your dog figure out that you want him to pick up his paw and put it in your hand when you say, "Shake!"?) Can dogs solve problems? (Can a dog figure out how to get his mouth on that food you've got?)

Sometimes the answer is yes. Dogs do, for example, understand that unseen or unsmelled things exist. If a treat is covered with a cup, dogs knock the cup right over and gobble up the reward. In other tests, dogs show that they can tell the difference between *large* and *small*—if offered a small pile of food and a large pile, they have no trouble choosing the larger one (especially if one pile is a good bit larger than the other). Dogs have even learned how to use a simple tool—pulling a string—to get a biscuit attached to that string.

But dogs don't pass all the tests. They make lots of mistakes when offered a choice between a pile of three biscuits and a pile of four, or a pile of five and seven. When the piles are quite similar, the difference between *large* and *small* doesn't seem clear enough for dogs to notice. For some reason, dogs develop a liking for one of the two piles and continue to go to the same one time after time—no matter if it's bigger or smaller. This leads to even more mistakes.

Dogs *can* find hidden food, but they get worse and worse at the job as the hiding gets more complicated. And their ability to use tools—like that string—has limits. If they are shown *two* strings, they will usually pull the nearest one, whether it's attached to a biscuit or not. It is as if dogs can understand an idea like *Pull string! Get biscuit!* but not an idea as complicated as *The biscuit is attached to this string (not that one), and if the right string is pulled, the biscuit will be closer and I can eat it.*

If you were rating your dog on these intelligence tests, he might come out more "dim but happy" than "top of the obedience class." Is that the answer? Is the dog just . . . not that smart?

Actually, the problem lies more with the *tests* than with the dogs' intelligence. A closer look at all of these tests reveals a problem. Without meaning to, the researchers have rigged their tests against dogs.

Consider this common experiment, for example. A dog is being held by a leash. A researcher shows the dog a great new toy. This dog *loves* new toys. The researcher then puts the toy in a bucket, making sure the dog can see. She takes the bucket behind a screen. Then she comes back out from behind the screen with the bucket.

She shows the bucket to the dog. It is empty.

It's not a cruel joke, really. It's an attempt to see if the dog understands what has happened when an object has been moved while out of sight. Does the dog think that the toy has vanished because it is no longer in the bucket? Or does the dog understand that nothing can disappear into thin air? If the toy is not in the bucket, the only place it could be is behind the screen. Will the dog look behind the screen to find it?

Human children understand this idea before their second birthday. It's a commonly run test with animals, to see how they measure up to small humans. Hamsters, dolphins, cats, chimpanzees, and chickens have all been tested. So have dogs.

Some of these animals pass the test. Dogs? The results are mixed.

In a simple test, like the one I described above, dogs have no trouble looking behind the screen for the toy. But if the test gets more complicated, dogs don't do as well.

Suppose there are *two* screens. The researcher carries the toy-in-the-bucket behind screen #1 and comes out with an empty bucket. She shows the empty bucket to the dog. Then she walks behind screen #2 and comes out again. Where will the dog search for the toy now? Behind screen #1, where the toy clearly is, or behind screen #2, because that's where the person has just been?

Here dogs often fail. They race behind screen #2 to

check it out. They don't seem to understand that if the bucket was empty *before* the person went behind screen #2, the toy cannot possibly be behind screen #2.

Dogs aren't looking so smart here.

But it may be simply that dogs don't think about their toys the way small human beings do. Dogs (and wolves, too) have a fairly simple relationship with objects in their environment. They eat them or they play with them. They don't need to spend a lot of time contemplating them. Dogs like toys, sure, and they know when a special toy is missing. But they don't usually mull over all the possible stories for what happened to that toy. They simply start looking for it, or wait for it to show up again.

Maybe this is why dogs don't seem to think carefully about which screen the toy is behind. Or maybe there's another reason.

Here's another experiment to consider. Show your dog a ball, and then hide it from him under one of two cups. Make sure your dog doesn't see which cup the ball went under. If your dog can't smell the ball, and if he's got no clues about which cup is hiding it, he'll look under either cup at random. A logical approach. We'd do the same if we had no clues.

But suppose you give your dog a clue. Let him peek under the cup with the ball. Now he knows where it is, and once he's allowed to search, he'll go straight for the right cup. That's not surprising.

But suppose you give your dog a different kind of clue. Suppose you let him peek under the *wrong* cup, the cup where the ball isn't. Then let him try to find the ball. Will he go for the right cup? Will he figure out that if the ball *isn't* under the cup you showed him, it must be under the other one?

He won't. He'll go right for the empty cup first.

Does that mean dogs are, well, a bit dim?

Or does it mean dogs are focused not on cups and balls, or toys and screens, but on something else? On *people*?

Dogs, as we have seen, pay a lot of attention to people. They are *good* at paying attention to people. When they are given a problem to solve, dogs cleverly look to us. As far as dogs are concerned, the things that human beings do are important, full of information. (One reason for this, of course, is that our actions often lead to dogs getting food.)

If a person flips over a cup, a dog will be interested in *that cup* (whether it has a ball under it or not). If an experimenter ducks behind screen #2, a dog will be interested in *that screen*. The dog's attention goes where the human's attention goes. These experiments don't necessarily prove that dogs are not smart. They prove that dogs have learned to keep their eyes, and their attention, on human beings.

If the researcher keeps this truth about dogs in mind, dogs do much better on the tests. If you show your dog an empty cup, but then put your hands on the other cup as well, your dog is more likely to figure the problem out. He'll realize that the ball is not under the empty cup, and he'll search for it under the right one.

In one experiment, wolves and dogs were tested to see which did better at getting food out of a locked box. Wolves seemed to beat the dogs at this task. They would keep at it until they got their mouths on the food. Maybe they figured out how to open the box, or maybe they just kept trying and trying until something worked.

Dogs, on the other hand, would try for a while. Then, once it became clear that the box would not open easily, they'd move on. Dogs would come up to the researcher and try something else: getting his attention and begging until the person gave in and opened the box.

At first glance, it seemed that wolves solved the puzzle and dogs failed. But wait—did the dogs fail? No. They just used a tool that the wolves didn't know about: *us*. Wolves used their teeth and paws to open the box. Dogs used a person.

Dogs have learned that human beings are useful for all sorts of things. We're protectors, food-givers, company. We solve the puzzles of closed doors and empty water dishes. We can untangle leashes from trees or give dogs things to chase and chew. How handy a human being is to have around! It's a clever strategy for a dog with a problem to turn to a human being for help.

So are dogs smart? They are smart at using us. They are very good at getting human beings to do the things that they need.

LEARNING FROM OTHERS

Yesterday Pump learned, by walking through the doors of a pet supermarket, that when you walk toward walls, they open up and let you through. Today she unlearned it, painfully.

Once dogs solve a problem—discover where a treat is hidden, learn how to open a closed door—they get it. They have noticed how things are (a treat is out of reach), figured out what to do (go over to a human and whine), and realized the connection (then the human will get the treat and hand it over).

Dogs will apply what they have learned over and over again. If you hand a dog a biscuit for sitting politely, expect to see him sitting politely a lot. Sometimes dogs learn things we wish they hadn't. A dog who jumps up on the counter once to find out where that delicious smell of cheese is coming from is likely to be up on the counter many times after that.

There is no doubt that dogs can learn. But learning is a complicated thing, depending on who is doing the learning. It can mean something as simple as understanding the command "Sit!" Or it can mean memorizing a scene from Shakespeare or understanding algebra.

Dogs might not be able to memorize Shakespeare or pass math tests. But they *can* learn "Sit!" They can learn a lot of other things too.

A dog's wolfish ancestors had to learn to hunt in order to survive. But most of what we ask dogs to learn has very little to do with food. We ask dogs to change position ("Sit!" "Jump up!" "Lie down!" "Roll over!"), to act in a very specific way about a particular object ("Get my shoes," "Get off the bed!"), to start or stop what they're doing ("Wait," "No!" "Okay"), to change their moods ("Cool it!" "Go get him!"), to move toward us or away from us ("Come!" "Go away!" "Stay!").

Learning "Sit!" or "Stay!" may not seem like rocket

science, but surely these commands must be bizarre and bewildering to a dog. Nothing in an animal's life prepares it for being asked to lower its rump to the ground and hold it there until you say it can stop. And yet dogs learn to do what we ask, even when the actions must make no sense at all from their point of view. When you think about it, it is pretty remarkable that dogs can learn to do this kind of thing at all.

PUPPY SEE, PUPPY DO

One morning, as I woke up lying on my belly, I pulled my arms over my head, stretched my legs into pointed toes, and pulled myself up onto my forearms. Next to me, Pump stirred and matched me move for move. She stretched her front legs, straightened her back legs, and pulled herself upright. Now we greet each other every morning with matching stretches. Only one of us swings her tail.

We know that dogs can learn commands. But can they learn merely by watching others—by example?

Human beings imitate each other all the time. We stare at each other to figure out what to wear, how to act, and how to react to things that happen. If I see you opening a can with a can opener just once, I can probably do it myself. (At least I hope so.)

Imitating someone else might seem simple, but it is actually a fairly complex mental activity. To imitate successfully, you must see what someone else is doing (putting the can opener on the can), understand why they are doing it (to get at the stuff that's inside), and figure out how you can do the same actions with your own hands.

Dogs are not true imitators when it comes to can openers. Your dog may have watched you open hundreds of cans and never once tried it himself. But this isn't a fair comparison, you might say. Dogs don't have thumbs. Their paws are not made to open cans.

Your complaint would be fair. So the question becomes, can dogs be taught, by imitation, to do a new *dog* thing?

Watch dogs interact for ten minutes and you'll see plenty of behavior that looks like imitation. One dog flaunts a gloriously big stick, and another finds a stick of his own and flaunts it back. If one dog finds a spot for digging, another may soon join him at the growing hole. One dog's discovery that he can swim might lead others to splash in. By watching others, dogs learn the special pleasures of mud puddles and of scrambling through bushes. Pump never uttered a sound until one of her dog companions started barking at squirrels. All at once, Pump was a barker, too.

The question is, is this real imitation? Sometimes animals do the same behavior not because they are imitating, but just because they are in the same place at the same time. Is that dog jumping into the lake because it sees the first dog doing it, and thinks it looks like a cool thing to do? Or is the dog simply drawn over to the edge of the water by the commotion the first dog is making, and once there, finds his own way into the water?

Does it matter which? Actually, it does. There is an important difference between the two behaviors.

Suppose I don't know how to open a door, and you do. If I watch you, I might see that you are doing something to the door, and it opens. Then I amble over to the door and kick it, hit it, and otherwise beat it up. I might get it to open too, by chance. But this wouldn't be real imitation.

If I imitated you, I would notice what you are doing with the door, and I would do exactly what you did—grab and turn the knob, push *after* the knob has been turned, and so on. I wouldn't kick or hit the door, because you didn't do that. And I'd behave this way because I'd understand that your actions (grabbing, turning, pushing) were connected to what you wanted—to leave the room through the open door.

Researchers wanted to find out if dogs were imitators like me watching you open the door, or more like that dog who just happened to wander over to the lake and ended up in the water. So they set up an experiment to see if a dog would imitate a human to get something that the dog wanted.

A toy or a bit of food was placed in the angle of a V-shaped fence. A dog was seated facing the point of that V, and was given a chance to get at the food.

The dog could not go straight over or through the fence. But he could go either left or right. There was no difference between the two directions; either one was as good as the other.

When the dogs were allowed to get the food on their own, they chose randomly between left and right. But then the experimenters changed the situation. Before the dog had a chance to get the food, the dog watched a person walk around the left side of the fence, talking to the dog all the while.

After that, the dogs chose the left side.

It looks as though the dogs were learning by imitation. And what they learned stuck, hard. When the experimenters changed the situation again, making a shortcut through the fence that the dogs could take, they ignored it. They kept on using the left route, the one they had learned by watching.

This experiment seemed to showed that dogs can see what others do (either humans or dogs) as a demonstration of how to get to a goal. But were they truly imitating? Or are dogs just likely to *follow that human* wherever that human goes?

One way to tell if a person or an animal is truly imitating is to see if he or she imitates only when there is a good reason to do so. In one experiment, infants watched an adult turn on a light switch in an unusual way—with his head. The researcher wanted to find out if the infants would imitate this behavior.

They did—but not always.

If the adult was carrying something in both hands when he head-butted the switch, the infants didn't use their heads to flip the switch. They could see that the man's hands were full. They knew their own hands were not full. They understood that they could use their hands to turn on the light—and so they did.

But if the adult had nothing in his hands and *still* used his head to turn on the light switch, then the infants were more likely to use their heads as well. They seemed to understand that there must be a good reason to turn on the switch in an unusual way, and that it might be worth trying it themselves. Infants, it seems, can tell when it might be worth their while to imitate, and when they don't need to bother.

Can dogs understand the same thing?

In a dog version of this experiment, one "demonstrator" dog was trained to press a wooden rod with his paw in order to make a treat pop out of a dispenser. Then the demonstrator dog performed his trick in front of other watching dogs. Sometimes the demonstrator dog pressed the rod with his foot while he was holding a ball in his mouth. Other times, he had no ball.

Then the watching dogs got a turn.

Before you hear what the watching dogs did, think a moment about how dogs usually approach their world. Using a paw to press something down is not the first thing most dogs try. Usually they go at the world mouth first, paws second. They will mouth a new object, bump it, knock into it. If they can, they will push it over, dig at it, or jump on it. But they do not usually consider things for a moment and then calmly press a rod with their foot.

But would they try that if they'd just watched another dog do the same thing?

They did. But *only* if the dogs saw that the demonstrator dog had good reason to use his paw.

If the demonstrator dog had *nothing in his mouth* while he pressed the rod with his paw, then the watching dogs also pressed the rod with their paws. They imitated exactly what the demonstrator dog had done.

If the demonstrator dog had a ball in his mouth when he pressed the rod with his paw, the watching dogs did not use their paws. They got the treat too—but they used their mouths to pull at the rod.

That the dogs imitated behavior this way is remarkable. They were not copying for the sake of copying. They were not simply going over to the wooden rod because another dog was there, and then accidentally pawing at the rod. They did exactly what the demonstrator dog did, placing a paw on the rod. And they did it *only* when they saw that the demonstrator dog must have had a good reason to use his paws instead of his mouth.

This looks very much like true imitation—understanding what the demonstrator is doing (getting a treat), figuring out how he is getting it (pressing a rod), and doing the same thing, but *just enough of the same thing* to get the treat.

It looks as if we can say that dogs are indeed able to learn by watching others, at least in certain situations—where food is at stake, for example. A final experiment suggests something even more impressive. One dog showed that he could imitate not just one action, but almost every new action he was asked to imitate. He seemed to understand what the idea of imitation means.

The dog in question, an assistant dog named Philip trained to work with blind people, had already learned to obey a number of commands. One was "turn around in a circle." Experimenters wondered whether he could do these actions not just on command, but after watching someone else do them. Sure enough, once Philip watched a human turn around and heard the command "Do it!," he turned in a circle. He imitated.

What would Philip do if the human he was watching did something completely new (and rather odd), such as running off to push a swing, tossing a bottle, or suddenly walking around another person and returning to the starting spot?

He did all those things when he heard the command "Do it!" It was as though Philip had learned not just to press a rod or turn in a circle, but to imitate on command. He seemed to understand that the command "Do it!" meant "Imitate what you see!"

This is not the final word on dogs and imitation. Just push a swing and ask your dog to imitate you, and you'll see that not all dogs understand imitation the same way. But it does suggest that dogs do not mindlessly copy what they see. Somehow, they think about what others are doing, why they are doing it, and what they need to do to get the same results—like making a treat pop out of a dispenser.

Dogs may be naturally good imitators, partly because

they are such good watchers. By nature, they look at us, and what they see allows them to learn from what we do. That is what I see when Pump stretches herself beside me in the morning.

THEORY OF MIND

I open the door quietly and Pump's there, not two feet away. She stops in her tracks and looks over her shoulder at me, her ears down, her eyes wide. There is something in her mouth. As I come closer, she wags low, ducks her head, and then I see what she has—the cheese. The entire enormous piece of cheese that I set out on the counter earlier. She gulps twice and it's gone, down the gullet.

Think of the dog caught in the act of stealing food from the table. When I saw Pump with her mouth full of cheese, and I realized that she had seen me, I knew she was about to make a move to get that cheese into her stomach. When she looked back at me, did she know I was going to try to stop her?

I can't help thinking that she did know. The moment I opened that door and she looked at me, we both knew what the other was going to do.

But can it be proved?

This is the most complex kind of problem that the

study of animal behavior can tackle. It raises questions of whether an animal can think of others as independent creatures with their own, separate minds. When an animal or a human being can do this, we say that he or she has a "theory of mind."

You may never even have heard of a theory of mind, but chances are that you have one yourself—a very advanced one. You understand that other people can know things that you don't. (Your teacher knows more about science than you do.) You also understand that you might know things other people don't. (You hid the last Hershey's bar from your sister so now she doesn't know where it is.) You realize that it is possible for another person to understand the world in a way different than the way you understand it.

If you *didn't* have a theory of mind, everyday events would be entirely confusing. Imagine that someone is coming toward you, mouth wide, waving a hand high in the air. If you have a theory of mind, you start imagining what is causing the stranger to act this way. Is he trying to say hello? Does he need help? Without a theory of mind, the person's behavior would simply be baffling.

Human babies are not born with a theory of mind, but if their brains develop normally, they acquire one. It seems that the process of development happens naturally, simply by doing the things babies naturally do—watching others and paying attention to *their* attention.

And what about dogs? Do they have a theory of mind?

When your dog looks you in the face, does he know there is a mind behind that face, thinking its own thoughts? Does your dog understand that you may know things that he doesn't? Or that he may know things you don't?

Here's what one dog, Philip (remember him from the imitation test?), found waiting for him at home one day. Usually his favorite tennis balls were scattered all over the house. This day, every ball in the house had been collected, and a lot of people were standing about looking at him.

Fine so far. Philip (who had no idea he was the subject of an experiment) didn't freak out. But he might have been a bit confused when, one by one, his balls were shown to him and then placed into a first, a second, or a third box. Then the boxes were locked.

This was new stuff for Philip. Was it a game? Was it a trick? Whatever was happening, he could see that his balls were being put somewhere other than his favorite place—right inside his mouth.

When his owner let him go, Philip, naturally, went straight toward a box where he saw a ball hidden. He nuzzled the box. This turned out to be the right thing to do, since it made the humans say loud, happy words, open the box, and give him the ball.

But the people around Philip kept taking his balls away and putting them back in the boxes. So he kept playing along. Then they started locking the boxes and putting the key elsewhere. This made the whole thing take longer.

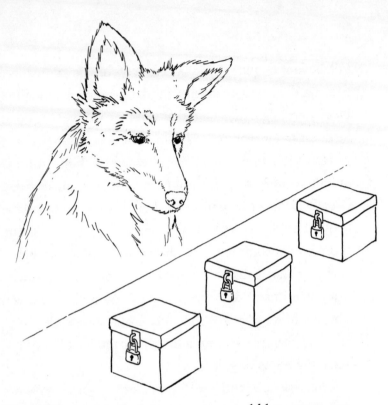

After Philip nuzzled a box, someone would have to go get the key, unlock the box, and hand him the ball.

Finally, one person put a ball in a box, locked the box, placed the key somewhere away from the box, and left the room. Then a second person came in. This was not Person #1, who had hidden the ball in the box. But surely Person #2, like all the other people, would be able to use that key-thing to open the box-thing and get the ball where it belonged, in Philip's mouth.

This was the moment the experimenters had been waiting for. They wanted to know how Philip saw Person #2 in the room. Would Philip realize that Person #2 might

ALEXANDRA HOROWITZ

not know where the key was? Could a dog understand that his own mind might hold a piece of information (the location of the key) that another person's mind did not?

The experiment was tried over and over. Over and over, Philip looked at the place where the key had been put, or he moved toward the key. He used his eyes and his body as communication, giving Person #2 the information that was needed to open the box.

Did Philip know what he was doing? Was he just looking toward that key because he knew it would open the box, and he really wanted that box open? Or because a person had just been handling that key and dogs tend to pay attention to what human beings are doing? His gaze *did* tell Person #2 where the key was, but perhaps that was only an accident. How could the researchers be sure?

They came up with a way to answer that question. They tried the experiment in two different ways. In one version, the person with Philip *had seen* the key being placed in its location. In this case, Philip looked at the key less often. In the second version, the person with Philip *had not seen* the key being put down. Here, Philip looked at the key more often. He seemed able to understand the difference between a person who needed to be told where the key was, and a person who already knew.

Philip could tell the difference between two different minds with different information inside them. He seemed to have a theory of mind.

Philip is only one dog, and maybe he is particularly clever. Other experiments trying to figure out if dogs have a theory of mind have had mixed results. Sometimes dogs seem to be showing that they are thinking about what others might know. Sometimes they show the opposite.

All these experiments, though, must be rather bizarre for the dogs. The dogs patiently endure people who take their balls away and put them in locked boxes over and over again. In other experiments they encounter people with blindfolds or buckets on their heads. No doubt we often do things (staring at flat screens, talking into small boxes) that our dogs do not understand, but these experiments must be particularly strange.

Suppose, instead of setting up a baffling experiment, we simply look at dogs doing what they do—playing with other dogs. This is why I spent a year watching dogs play in living rooms and veterinary offices, down hallways and pathways, on beaches and in parks. Perhaps what I saw could tell me whether dogs have a theory of mind. Could I show that, as dogs play, they are thinking about the minds of other dogs?

MINDS AT PLAY

Pump appears in the corners of all the videos. In one, she hops nimbly to avoid crashing into a dog who is coming toward her too fast, and then chases after him. In another, she lies next

ALEXANDRA HOROWITZ

to another dog as they pretend to bite, mouths wide. In a third, she tries and fails to join two dogs in play. As they run off together she is left wagging alone.

Rough-and-tumble play between two strong dogs is a marvel to watch. The playing dogs seem to greet each other briefly, and then, all of a sudden, attack. Teeth are bared. They jump on and over each other, bodies tangled. If they hear a noise nearby, they may both stop, perfectly quiet. It only takes a look or a paw raised in the air to begin the wrestling again.

Play may just seem like *something dogs do*, nothing remarkable. But when it comes to science, we have a strict definition of play.

Play is something animals do because they want to. (Nobody *has* to play.) When they play, animals use behaviors familiar from their everyday life. A dog wrestles with another dog, as he would in a real fight. A cat bats a ball, as she would if she were hunting a mouse. But actions in play are not quite the same as they are in the animal's non-playing life. They may be drawn out or cut short, they may be rough or gentle, they may be done over and over. Play draws from real life, but is all in fun.

Scientists don't define play this carefully in order to take all the fun out of it. We define it so that we are sure we can recognize it. All sorts of actions can be play: Otters slide, dogs chase, kids play tag. But if we have a definition in mind, we can see that play is what they are all doing.

Why do animals play? It's a bit of a puzzle. Most of the time, to figure out why an animal is doing something, we try to see how the behavior helps an animal survive, find food, or raise young. Play doesn't seem to do any of these things. At the end of playtime, no food has been hunted, no territory kept safe from intruders, no mate found. Instead, two dogs collapse panting to the ground, wagging their tongues at each other.

Play is hard work. It takes a lot of energy. Players can get hurt if the play goes wrong. So there must be some real benefit to play, some way in which it helps animals survive, or they would not spend so much time and energy on a risky activity.

We just don't quite know what that benefit might be.

It may be that play teaches skills that animals need in their non-playing lives. Maybe play helps animals learn to handle unexpected events—after all, it does seem animals seek out play that offers surprises. Human children need play for their minds to develop normally. Perhaps it is the same for some animals. Or perhaps play is simply what animals do if they have extra energy and time.

Play among dogs is particularly interesting because they play more than any of their relatives, including wolves. And it isn't just puppies who play—adults dogs do it too. This is rare among adult animals. Most playing animals, even humans, give up play when they grow up. Adult humans sometimes play team sports or spend hours with their video games, but they don't usually tackle or tag their friends and then run. Adults tend not to make faces at other adults and then collapse in laughter.

In my study of dog play I followed dogs with a video camera at parks and beaches. After a few hours of fun the dogs would be packed into cars and I would walk home. I'd sit down in front of my computer and play back the videos at an extremely slow speed. My camera could capture thirty images every *second*, and I looked at every one.

I could see exactly what dogs do when they play.

The rough-and-tumble play of dogs that I was watching is a social event, something they do together. Playing animals notice each other. They have to, or the play won't work. Dogs take turns when they play, which means each has to see when it's time for his turn to chase or lead to be over and the other dog's turn to start. Stronger dogs will even make things easy for weaker, younger, or slower partners. They might throw themselves on the ground, move more slowly, bite more gently. All of this means dogs must be aware of how much their play partners can do.

There were two behaviors of this social play that I was particularly interested in: play signals and attention-getters. We've already noticed attention-getters—barks, whines, bumps, nudges. They're obvious (they're supposed to attract attention, after all). They are meant to be sensed (heard, seen, felt) by someone whose attention the dog would like to have.

An attention-getter can be a dog putting his body in front of someone's gaze, as when your dog sticks his head between you and the book you're holding. Some are meant to be heard, like a bark. If those fail, physical contact might work—a paw on the lap, a bump with the hip, a light bite on the rump.

Some attention-getters work better than others. One move that works quite well is what I call an *in-your-face*, when one dog gets its body very close to the face of another dog. But it doesn't work if the dog whose attention you want is busy playing with a third dog. Then something else is needed, which explains those dogs who circle a playing pair for minutes, barking and barking.

Play signals are what makes play between dogs work. They are a way to ask another dog to play or just to announce that you're ready if anybody else is. If we put them into human words, the signals might translate to, *Let's play* or *I want to play with you* or even *Ready? Because I'm about to play with you!*

Play signals are not just good manners for dogs; they are necessary. Dog play is rough. If you are biting another dog, tackling that dog's legs, or jumping on top of him, you'd better be sure that dog knows you are playing, not fighting. With a play signal, a bite is part of the game. Without one, a bite is just a bite.

Nearly every bout of play begins with one of these signals.

The most typical play signal is the *play bow*. A dog bows low on his forelegs, his rump in the air, his mouth open and relaxed, tail high and wagging. This dog is pulling out all the stops to coax someone into play. Even though you don't have a tail, you can try this play signal yourself. Expect your dog to respond happily with a play bow in return, or a friendly nip, or at least a second look.

Two dogs who know each other well can use a shortened form. There's the *play slap*, when the front legs clap on the ground; it's like the beginning of the play bow, no bothering with the end. Or there's the *open mouth display*, the mouth open without the teeth bared, or the *head bow*, just a quick bob of the head with the mouth open. Even panting in quick bursts can be a signal to play.

As I watched my videos, I studied just how these bumps, barks, and bows of play were used. Did dogs use attention-getters all the time? Or did they use them only when they really needed to get their play partners' attention? Did they use any play signal at any time? Or did they use a signal that was just right for the partner they wanted to play with?

Dog play happens so quickly that it's hard to give a clear account of what goes on. You might see two dogs at play and describe it this way: *Bailey and Darcy ran around together ... Darcy chased Bailey and barked ... they both bit at each other's faces ... then they split up.* ... But this misses a lot. It doesn't tell us how often Darcy and Bailey made the play easier for their partner, throwing themselves on the ground, on their backs, letting themselves be bitten. It doesn't tell us whether they took turns biting and being bitten, or chasing and being chased. And most importantly, it doesn't tell us if Darcy and Bailey used play signals with each other when those signals could be seen and responded to.

But by slowing my videos down, I could find all of these details. What I discovered was remarkable.

The dogs I watched used play signals only at very particular times. They always signaled at the beginning of play, and always to a dog who was looking at them. They were not using their play signals randomly. They were using them at the right times and aiming them at the right dogs.

During playtime, dogs get easily distracted, turning their attention away from their play partners. One might find a ripe smell underfoot. Another might turn his head to check out a new dog coming near. A third dog might look for his owner. When this happens, play pauses briefly. For it to start up again, a dog has to catch his distracted partner's attention and perform a play signal. Dogs also play-signaled when both had taken a break from play and one wanted to start up again. Each time, they signaled to dogs who could see them.

My videos show that these dogs were using play signals to communicate, and they were doing it on purpose. When they signaled to animals who could see their movements, they showed that they were thinking about the minds of their audience.

They showed this in other ways as well.

If one dog became distracted during play, his partner might have chosen to play-bow over and over, hoping to lure him back to play. But this is not what the dogs did. Instead, they used an attention-getter *before* doing a bow. More remarkably, they used just the right attention-getter, one that showed they understood just how distracted their partner had become.

If the play partner was only a bit distracted, the dog would use a mild attention-getter. They'd get close to the dog's face—using the *in-your-face*. Or they'd jump backward: an *exaggerated retreat*. It was similar to the way you might wave *hello?* in front of a daydreaming friend.

But if the other dog was *very* distracted, looking away or even playing with another dog, stronger attention-getters were needed. Then the first dog would try bites, bumps, or barks. These choices showed dogs who could tell just how distracted their partners were, and just the kind of attention-getter that was needed to start play up again.

Then, once they had their partner's attention back, the dogs did a play bow or another play signal. They did not do it the other way around—try a play signal and *then* an attention-getter. They only used the play signal once their partner's attention was where it belonged—on them. This is just what animals with a theory of mind do. They think about someone else's state of attention and talk only to those who can hear and understand them.

Not all dogs show the same behavior. Some dogs don't seem to think hard about their attention-getters. They bark, and if that gets no response, they bark and bark some more. Others use attention-getters when attention has already been gotten, or play signals when play has already been signaled. This might mean that dogs do have a theory of mind, but not quite the same one that humans have.

Dogs are probably more interested in playing than they are in thinking about thinking. They may have a beginning of an understanding of other's minds—just enough to allow play to go ahead. This may be all that they need.

If your dog does have a theory of mind, does it mean

that he is interested in what you might be thinking? No, not necessarily. Maybe your mind is occupied with the score in a basketball game or when your best friend is going to text. Your dog probably doesn't know a thing about that.

On the other hand, does it mean that your dog might understand on some basic level that what you do, your behavior, can show him what's on your mind? Yes. Dogs are used to communicating with human beings, and they are good at it. Understanding that your mind holds information, and that your behavior gives him clues about that information, is part of what makes dogs good at being with humans.

WHAT HAPPENED TO THE CHIHUAHUA

Remember the Chihuahua from the beginning of this book? The one who was playing with the wolfhound? Now that we have learned more about dogs and play, we can look back at what happened between them.

The wolfhound did a play bow, rump high in the air, making it perfectly clear that he wanted to play with the little dog, not eat her. The Chihuahua bowed in return, accepting the offer. In the language of dogs, this is enough for the two of them to see each other as equals, as partners in play.

Then the wolfhound took steps to make himself the Chihuahua's equal. He threw himself to the ground, putting himself at her level, leaving himself open to her attacks. The huge benefits of his size and weight vanished. He made it possible for a tiny dog to play with a giant one.

They bumped and jostled. They bit. Every bite was matched with a play signal, to show that this wasn't a fight. Every bite was gentle. No one got hurt. When the hound hit the little dog too hard, sending her scurrying back, it might have seemed like the big dog saw the small one as fleeing prey. But he didn't. And to show the Chihuahua it was all in fun, the wolfhound took a step back and offered a play slap, a milder version of the play bow. The slap said, again, that this is play, not fighting. It worked. The Chihuahua rushed right back into his face.

Finally, when the hound was pulled away by his owner, the Chihuahua barked to get his attention. If the wolfhound had turned around, we might have seen the Chihuahua open her mouth or leap a tiny leap—play signals showing her hope of continuing the game with her enormous friend.

9

INSIDE OF A DOG

In everything Pump does, I see her personality. It's there in the way she hesitates to climb the steep steps into the park—but once at the top, plunges bravely ahead. It's in the joy she takes in running and rolling, in her (momentary) delight at my return from a long trip. It's in the way she checks back with me on walks, but keeps a few paces apart from me. She needs me, but she has a self that is just her own, an independence. She has her own pace of life.

Science can tell us how dogs see, smell, hear, look, and learn. But what about the personalities of dogs? Their feelings? The way they experience life? Can science tell us what we want most to know—what do dogs think about?

It's not easy to find out. But we can use the facts and information that science has collected to think about two questions:

What does a dog know?
What is it like to be a dog?

WHAT A DOG KNOWS

Let's start with the ways dogs approach the world (nose first), the remarkable attention they pay to human beings, and what we know about how dogs learn. Then we might be able to figure out what dogs can know. What do dogs know about time, about themselves, about right and wrong, about emotions, about life and death?

What Dogs Know About Time

I arrive back home. Pump gives me a quick greeting and then races off. While I was gone she found all the biscuits I left around the house for her, and she has been waiting until now to eat them. She gobbles one that is balanced on the edge of a chair, one off a doorknob, and then snags the tricky one left on top of a pile of books.

Do animals know that time is passing? Surely they do. You cannot exist one moment to the next without experiencing that time is going by. But does your dog experience time in the same way that you do? Does he sense the passage of a day?

Dogs may not be about to speak the word "day," or

even to think it, but they must have some concept about what a day is. We give it to them. We organize their days, from getting-up time to going-out time to eating time. And we give them plenty of clues about landmarks in that day. When we go into the kitchen and start opening the fridge or rattling bowls and plates, it's dinnertime. If we call the dog's name, all doubt is over—it's time to eat.

But what if we took away all those clues? If the dog couldn't see or hear us getting dinner ready, even if all hints from light and dark were gone, dogs would still know that it's time to eat.

They don't wear watches, but dogs do have a clock—one that is inside their brains. Like human beings and many other animals, dogs have a part of the brain that governs sleep, waking, and hunger, keeping all on a regular schedule. Responding to this natural clock, dogs are most active at dawn and then settle down to rest in the afternoon, with another burst of energy in the evening.

> She is patient. How she waits for me. She waits as I duck into the local grocery store. She waits at home, warming the bed, the chair, the spot by the door, until I return. She waits for me to finish up what I'm doing before we go outside, for me to finish talking with the friend I meet on our walk; for me to figure out when she is hungry. She waited for me to learn where she

liked to be rubbed. And for me to begin, at last,
to figure her out.

It's likely that your dog, with the clock inside his brain, knows just how long a day is. But if so, a horrible thought occurs—are dogs terribly bored, waiting all day alone at home?

How can we tell if a dog is bored? First we need to figure out what boredom is.

Scientists have not spent much time studying boredom. But if we think about it, we can recognize what boredom feels like and how we show it. Boredom is a lack of interest in what is around us. We know when we are bored, and we can guess when others are bored. We see their energy lagging. They don't do much, except for repeating small movements endlessly: thumbs twiddling, feet tapping. Their attention wanders away.

We can look for these kinds of behaviors in dogs. Less energy means less moving, more lying and sitting. Nothing to pay attention to may just mean settling into sleep. Dogs don't have thumbs to twiddle, but they pace. So do animals in zoos. Zoo animals without enough to do or think about may also lick or chew on the same patch of skin, pull out feathers or fur, rub their ears or faces, or rock back and forth.

So is your dog bored? If you return home to find socks, shoes, or underwear strewn across your house, or

ALEXANDRA HOROWITZ

yesterday's garbage all over the kitchen floor, there's a simple answer—yes, your dog was bored. So he found himself something to do.

If you'd like to keep your clothes unchewed and the garbage in the trash can, the best idea is to give your dog something to do while you are gone. And take note of how he looks on your return. Usually, even if they've been waiting for us awhile, our dogs are healthy and look well when we get back. We get away with leaving them—with boring them—because they take comfort in habit, in knowing what to expect. Your dog can come to know that you'll be gone for a while, and that you'll be back. And he'll be there to meet you, tail wagging. Dogs may even know how long they must spend waiting until you show up again.

That is why I leave more treats hidden around my apartment for Pump the longer I'll be gone. I'm telling her I'll be away, and giving her something to do while I'm gone.

What Dogs Know about Themselves

The best scientific tool we have come up with to see if animals truly think about themselves is the mirror. When a researcher placed a mirror outside of chimpanzees' cages, they first tried to threaten or attack the image in the glass. After a few days, the chimps started to do new things in the mirrors. They picked their teeth. They blew bubbles. They made faces. They looked at parts of their bodies they could ordinary never see—the rump, inside the mouth, up the nostrils.

But did the chimps truly realize that the images in the mirror were images of themselves? The researcher tried to find out. He sneakily placed a dot of red ink on the chimp's foreheads, so that the chimps didn't know it was there. Then the researcher watched to see what the marked chimps would do when they saw themselves in the mirror again. Guess what? They touched the spot on their own heads, just as you would probably do. Then the chimps brought their hands down to examine the ink with their mouths (probably *not* what you would do).

The chimps knew that the red mark on the mirror image was in fact on their own heads. This seems to mean that chimps are able to think about themselves. They looked at the chimp in the mirror, and they understood that the chimp in the mirror was the same chimp who was doing the looking. They'd passed the test.

The mirror test has been done on many other chimpanzees, on dolphins (who moved their bodies to examine the mark), on magpies (who try to get the mark off), and on at least one elephant (who touched the mark with her trunk). It has been done on monkeys, who showed no interest in the mark. And dogs? Dogs have not passed the test either. They do not seem to care about a mark on the fur of the dog in the mirror.

Why not?

Maybe dogs can't think about themselves. Maybe they see the moving picture in the mirror as just that—a picture. A picture of a dog, perhaps. But not a reflection of the dog who is doing the looking.

Or perhaps the mirror test is not a good one for an animal who relies most of all on the nose. The image in the mirror, after all, doesn't have a *smell*. Maybe a dog cannot think of an image without a smell as himself. Finally, maybe dogs just don't care that much about marks on their bodies. A dog isn't interested in why the tip of his black tail is white, or what color his new leash is. He may not care about a mark on his head either.

Are there any behaviors in a dog's normal life that might show that they think about themselves?

Most of the time, dogs seem to know some things about themselves—what they can or cannot do, for instance. A dog who loves sticks tends to pick up sticks the right size for his mouth—not too big to be lifted, not so small that they disappear down his throat. A dog used to playing with other dogs will change how he plays depending on the size of his play partners. Big dogs know to treat small dogs more gently, and might even flop down (as the wolfhound did with the Chihuahua) to let themselves be attacked. Older dogs also play differently with puppies, who haven't yet learned the rules of play.

What about those tiny dogs who strut up to big dogs, ears up, tails high? "He thinks he's a big dog," owners often say. But it's more likely that the little dog knows his own size quite well. He is making up for his smallness with his body language, announcing his other qualities as loudly as he possibly can.

And what about a giant dog who loves to squeeze into a lap? "He thinks he's small," his owner may sigh. But the dog probably simply likes to be touched, on as much of his body as he can manage. He'll sit in a lap as long as his owner will put up with it, and then go find a dog-sized pillow to sit on elsewhere.

If we look at all the evidence, we see that dogs know at least some things about themselves. They have a sense of their own size and their own strength. They know what they can or cannot do.

Or think about working dogs, who spend their days with animals who are not dogs. Sheepdogs do not grow up to act like sheep. They do not bleat or chew their cud or butt heads with other sheep. In fact, they tend to do the opposite—they treat sheep like dogs. Sheepdogs will growl at a sheep, for example. Growling is a dog noise, not a sheep one. Dogs who spend all day around other animals do not start to copy the way those other animals behave. They know they are dogs.

So could we say that when they are not playing, fetching sticks, or herding sheep, dogs sit around thinking, *My, but I'm a fine medium-size dog, aren't I?* No, they don't. As far as we know, it's only human beings who spend this amount of time thinking about who we are. But dogs do seem to know at least something about what it means to be a dog, and more particular, to be themselves. It means they can carry a stick about *that* big, no bigger. It means they'd better ease up if they're playing with a dog half their size. It means they don't bleat like a sheep. Something inside a dog's head tells it what it means to be himself.

Dog Years, Past and Future

Can dogs remember things? Definitely. Your dog remembers who you are when you return home. He knows where his favorite toy was left and what time dinner is supposed to be delivered. He can remember friends and enemies, a shortcut to the park, and where the good peeing posts are.

But there is more to memory than keeping track of things and places, other people, and other dogs. People think about their memories, about what has happened to us in the past. Our minds also drift forward, and we start to imagine what might happen to us in the future. What we remember about the past and dream about the future makes up a big part of who we are.

Do dogs think like this? Does a dog remember being a puppy? Can he recall the first time he met you? Does he think about the events in his life as *his* events in *his* life? Is a dog's memory a part of what it means to be that dog?

We don't know very much yet about how and what

dogs can remember. But we do know language is a big part of our own memory, and dogs don't have language. When events happen to us, we put them into words, and we turn the words into stories that we tell to our family and repeat to ourselves. (This explains why we don't usually have clear memories of life before we were about three years old. We were not good at using language then; we didn't have the words to think about our experiences. And so we don't remember the things that happened to us.)

So if dogs don't use words, does it mean they cannot remember? This clearly can't be right. Pumpernickel did not eat up the treats I left for her right away; she waited until I came home. But she remembered where each treat was. Dogs remember ground that was rough underfoot, and they stay away from it. They remember dogs who suddenly turned fierce and people who acted cruelly, and they stay away from them too.

Dogs also show that they remember people and dogs they meet. They recognize their owners, of course. They also come to know people who visit their owners often. They play best with dogs they have met many times before, and they develop their own play signals to use with these dogs. Longtime playmates need only do a shorthand version of a play bow before diving into full play.

What about the future? If dogs know at least something about the things that have happened to them in the past, do they know anything about things that might happen in the future?

There isn't yet much evidence to figure this out. But we can certainly say that dogs have a sense of what might happen in the immediate future. Your dog will get excited if you take him on a familiar walk to the park or the pet food store. He'll get anxious on a car ride to the vet. He knows what's coming. But beyond that, we can't be sure how or even if a dog thinks about what his distant future is likely to hold.

Perhaps all we can say for certain now is that a dog hopes that tomorrow will be much like today—full of food, walks, and the company of his family.

What Dogs Know About Right and Wrong

When Pump was a young dog, this was a common scene in our house. I'd turn my back or go into another room. A fraction of a second later, Pump had her head in the kitchen trash can. If I returned and caught her, she'd immediately pull her nose out of the can. Her ears and tail would drop. She'd wag her tail while slinking away. Caught.

When researchers asked dog owners what their dogs knew about the world, most said that their dogs know when they have done something wrong. The owners believed that dogs have a category in their minds of *things one must never, ever do.* It's a category that includes tearing into the garbage, chewing up shoes, and snatching food off the kitchen counter.

You are probably familiar with the guilty look that I used to see on Pump's face after she'd been in the trash can. A dog trying to sneak out of the room with ears pulled back and pressed down against the head, tail wagging quickly and tucked between the legs, certainly looks like a dog who knows he's been caught red-pawed.

So does a dog with a nose in the trash *feel* guilty? Or is that look caused by something else? Maybe it's the excitement of sniffing the trash in the first place. Maybe it's the startled feeling of being discovered. Maybe it's the anxious feeling of knowing that your owner is about to make loud, unhappy noises.

Can dogs really know right from wrong?

Think about a two-year-old child who comes up to a table, gropes toward an expensive vase, and knocks it over. Does the child know that it is wrong to break things that belong to other people? Not really. She did not destroy the vase on purpose, to be mean, or to get back at someone. She is just an ordinary two-year-old still getting control of her own body, still learning that fragile things break when they fall down.

So are dogs like that two-year-old, without any understanding that chewing up the garbage is wrong? I designed an experiment to find out.

First, I needed something that dogs want—a bit of biscuit, a cube of cheese—in a place that a dog could reach. Next, I needed an owner who firmly told the dog, "No!" or "Leave it!" while pointing to the treat. The dogs had to understand that the bit of food that they wanted was off-limits.

Then the owner left the room.

The dog was in a room with the treat and another human being quietly running a video camera. Then one of two things happened: The dog obediently resisted eating the treat, or the dog gave in to temptation and ate it up.

Then the owner returned. If the dog was obedient, the owner was told so, and she greeted the dog with a happy hello. But if the dog ate the treat, the owner was told so and she scolded the dog—*No, Ella!*

Here's the tricky bit: Once in a while, I deceived the owner. I told her that the dog had been good, when he had not. Or that he had been bad, when he had been good. So sometimes the dog was unfairly punished, or greeted happily even though he did something wrong.

What I wondered was, how would the dogs behave in each of these cases?

Dogs who ate the forbidden treat could have modeled for that guilty look. They lowered their gaze, pressed their ears back, slumped their bodies, and turned their heads away. Sometime their tails wagged low between their legs.

But—and this is the important point—dogs who *did*

not eat the forbidden treat and who got scolded anyway looked just the same.

It didn't matter whether the dogs had disobeyed or not. They looked guilty either way. Why? Because their owners were angry with them. In fact, the innocent dogs who got scolded put on an extra-guilty look.

This experiment seems to tell us that a dog's classic guilty look has more to do with a scolding from the owner than the dog's own feelings about doing wrong. The dog may know that eating a forbidden treat means punishment, or the dog may simply be able to tell from the owner's posture, face, or voice that a scolding is on its way.

When the dog can sense that his owner is angry or displeased, he may look frightened. A dog who looks "guilty"—flat ears, slumped posture, and lowered tail—is showing signs of submission. A dog who looks like this is using his body to ask not to be punished. He isn't admitting that he's done wrong; he may not know what "wrong" means. He just knows that he needs to watch out when his owner looks or sounds like that.

What Dogs Know About Death

With age Pump uses her eyes less; she looks at me less.

With age she would rather stand than walk, rather lie down than stand. And so she lies next to me outside with her head between her legs,

ALEXANDRA HOROWITZ

nose still alert to the smells on the breeze.

With age she has become more stubborn. She insists on heaving herself up the stairs without help.

With age I have been given a gift. I understand more and more about the details of her life. As we do things together at her slower pace, I notice the regular smells she checks up on in the neighborhood. I feel how long she waits for me. I see how much she communicates to me simply by standing. I see her.

Every dog that you name and bring home will die. This fact is dreadful but absolutely true. It is part of what we accept when we share our lives with dogs.

It is less certain if dogs understand the fact that they will someday die. Did Pump notice when the old, droopy-eared dog down the block stopped coming out to play? Is she aware of her own stiffer walk, her graying fur? Does she notice that she sleeps more and plays less these days?

Human beings know that we cannot live forever. It is one of the things that makes us careful in life. We move back from the edge of the balcony. We buckle our seatbelts. We look both ways before crossing the street, and we don't jump into the tiger's cage. Do dogs do the same thing?

For the most part dogs pull away from danger. They move back from the balcony's edge or the rushing river, just as we do. They stay away from another animal that looks dangerous. They act to avoid death.

But every animal does this, right down to a paramecium, a little creature too tiny to see without a microscope, swimming around in a drop of water. Living things have an instinct to stay away from what will kill them. It doesn't mean that they are thinking about it.

But dogs do two things that are different from the paramecium. First, they act differently if they are hurt or dying. Dogs in serious trouble often work hard to move away from their families (either animal or human), to settle down, and perhaps die in a quiet spot. This behavior might show that they understand something about death— even just that it means they are vulnerable and need to be somewhere safe.

And second, dogs seem to understand when others are in danger of death.

Stories of so-called heroic dogs are always popping up in the news. A child lost in the mountains is kept alive by the warmth of dogs who stayed with him. A man who falls through the ice of a frozen lake is saved by the dog who came to the ice's edge. A dog barks at a boy about to put his hand into the den of a venomous snake, bringing the parents in time to save him.

Did these other dogs risk death on purpose to save the

people they loved? If they did, it could mean that some dogs understand what death is, know that they do not want their humans to die, and try hard to keep it from happening.

But we need to think a little more about these stories to be sure.

First, it's important to remember that the news tells us stories of things that are out of the ordinary. If a dog saves a lost hiker or a drowning child, that is remarkable. People want to know about it. If the opposite happens, it gets no attention. No one has ever written a newspaper headline that says LOST WOMAN DIES AFTER DOG FAILS TO FIND AND DRAG HER TO SAFETY!

Most dogs have never saved their owners from danger—not even once. The extraordinary actions of a few dogs here and there are interesting, but they don't prove much about dogs in general.

If we look at these stories of heroic dogs more closely, we can learn even more from them. For example, consider Norman.

Norman, a blind Labrador retriever, heard the screams of his family's children, caught in a river's current. The brother had managed to reach the shore, but the sister, Lisa, was struggling in the water. Norman jumped in and swam to Lisa. She grabbed his tail. Norman paddled for land, pulling Lisa with him, and they reached the shore together.

It looks like Norman understood that Lisa was in danger and took action to save her. But there is a simpler explanation.

If we think about Norman's story along with many other stories of dogs rescuing humans, we start to notice something they have in common. Again and again, dogs *came toward* the person who needed help, or *stayed close* to a person who needed rescue. Norman *swam toward* Lisa. The dogs *stayed with* the lost child on the mountain. In many cases, the dogs also drew attention to the person in trouble—barking, running around, creating a ruckus.

These are things that dogs do naturally. They are interested in people and stay close to them. They use attention-getting behaviors. If you are in trouble—lost, drowning, frightened—your dog can likely tell, because he knows you well and pays attention to you. Your trouble will make your dog anxious, and anxious dogs will bark, run around, or try to get close to you. These actions may well save you from drowning or bring helpful people to find you. If that happens, your dog will have saved your life.

So is Norman a hero? Of course. Did he *mean* to save Lisa from drowning? Did he know that she would die if he did not swim out to her and let her grab his tail? Probably not. At least we have no evidence that he did.

One clever experiment, in fact, shows that dogs do not always—or even usually—help in an emergency.

In this test, dog owners were asked to create a fake emergency. Some of them gasped, clutched their chests, and keeled over, as if they were having a heart attack. Some let a bookcase (made of very light wood) fall over on them, seeming to pin them to the ground as they yelled for help. In both cases, the dogs were nearby and so was a second person, a bystander—someone who could help the seeming victim.

What did the dogs do?

Some dogs came close to their owners. Sometimes they nuzzled and pawed at their bodies. Other dogs, however, just roamed around, wandering and sniffing the floor or the ground. Only a few dogs barked or went up to the second person nearby. And only one dog actually touched the bystander. This was a toy poodle, who jumped in the bystander's lap and settled down for a nap.

Not a single dog in this experiment did something that actually helped their owners. Not one actively tried to bring a second person over to help. This suggests that dogs (even Norman) simply do not understand what an *emergency* means. They do not know when someone is in danger of dying and what they must do to stop it from happening.

This isn't a perfect experiment. Maybe the dogs realized that the emergency wasn't real and that their owners were not really hurt or afraid. Dogs are good readers of us, after all. But certainly *something* was going on with their owners, silent on the floor or under the furniture, and the dogs did . . . nothing.

We can't blame dogs for not understanding an "emergency" the way we do. We might as well scold them for not knowing what *bicycle* or *mousetrap* means. Maybe, in fact, we can envy them. We know that one day we must lose our companions—they do not seem to know that one day they may lose us.

WHAT IS IT LIKE TO BE A DOG?

Can you know exactly what it feels like to be a dog? Can you experience the world as your dog experiences it?

Well, not quite. We can never know exactly what goes on inside a dog. But we can gather information and put together the best picture that we're able to.

We know a lot about how dogs' bodies work—how their eyes see, how their noses smell, how their brains put all this input together. We know about the wolflike ancestors that dogs came from. And we are gathering more and more knowledge about the things that dogs do.

When we put everything we know together, we have a pretty good picture of a dog's world: We have already seen that it is smelly, and it is full of very interesting people. It is also close to the ground. It is lickable. It either fits in the mouth or it doesn't. It is full of details, fleeting, and fast. It is written all over their faces. And it probably feels nothing like what it feels like to be us.

A Dog's World Is Close to the Ground

It's not something people think about much, and yet a dog's height is a huge part of what it means to be a dog. The head of an average dog, standing upright, is one to two feet off the ground. They live their lives at the level of an adult's knee. This explains a lot of their behavior—like *jumping on us.* If you don't want your dog to get a ball, you might hold it up by your head. What happens next? That's right. *Jumping up* is what happens when someone wants to get something that one needs to *jump up* to reach. Dogs love to greet our faces, but we don't bend down to see them. What happens? Yup.

Dogs aren't always jumping up, of course. They do find a lot down at ground level to be interested in. There are, for instance, lots of feet. Smelly feet. Our feet sweat a lot, especially when we are anxious or thinking hard. This makes our feet a very good source of the smells that, to our dogs, mean us.

Since our feet smell so interesting, it must be frustrating to dogs that we cover them up all the time. Those shoes! But then, of course, we take the shoes off, and shoes on the floor smell exactly like the person who has been wearing them. Plus they carry extra smells from whatever that person stepped on while walking outside. Socks are also wonderfully full of the smell of the people. No wonder your dog can sometimes be found with your socks in his mouth.

There are the legs of pants down there too, and long

skirts. Since dogs' eyes are so sensitive to motion, the way these things move as you walk must be tantalizing. It must be so tempting for a dog to take a quick nip or tug at the hem of your clothes. Maybe sometimes he does.

The world closer to the ground is also more smelly. Smells on the ground stay put, unlike smells in the air, which drift away. Things sound different down there too. Dogs might not hear much birdsong, up in the trees. But the way a fan makes the floor vibrate can disturb them. And loud sounds bounce easily off the floor and into a dog's ears.

A Dog's World Is Lickable

She is lying on the ground, head between paws, and notices something that might be interesting or edible a short stretch away on the floor. She pulls her head forward to it, her nose nearly but not quite *in* whatever has caught her attention. I can see her nostrils working as she figures out what the bit-of-something might be. She gives a wet snort, turns her head, and test-licks the spot with a quick swipe. Then she straightens up and sets to lick, lick, lick the floor with long strokes of her tongue.

To a dog, nearly everything is lickable. A spot on the floor, a spot on herself, a person's hand, toes, knees, face,

ALEXANDRA HOROWITZ

ears, or eyes, a tree trunk, a bookshelf, the car seat, the sheets, the floor, the walls. Everything.

Licking, which brings tiny bits of whatever is licked into the mouth, means that dogs are directly in contact with the world all of the time. They don't look at things from a safe distance; they don't poke them gently with a finger. They lick.

Dogs touch. They get close. You've probably seen this scene often on a sidewalk—two dog owners talking while their dogs strain at their leashes, trying to touch. Let them touch! Dogs greet strangers by getting into their space, not by staying out of it. Let them get into each other's fur, sniff deep, and mouth each other in greeting.

A Dog's World Either Fits in the Mouth or It's Too Big for the Mouth

If you enter a house and look around, you'll see that the space is full of furniture, books, pictures, clothes, toys, electronics—all things that you can do something with. You can sit on a couch, read a book, look at a picture, wear a shirt, play with a toy, switch on the TV.

A dog's world is the same as yours in one way—it is full of things that the dog can do something with. But the things that dogs do are not the same things that humans do. And so a dog's world is different from a human's.

For a dog, some things are chewed, some are eaten,

some are moved, some are sat upon, some are rolled in. To you, a pen is for writing, a teddy bear is for hugging, and a shoe is for wearing. To a dog, all of these things may be for picking up and carrying in the mouth.

There are also categories of things-that-move and thing-that-stand-still. To a dog, a running squirrel (good for chasing) may be an entirely different animal from a squirrel sitting still (not that interesting). A child holding a skateboard is not the same thing as a skateboarding child smoothly and quickly rolling down the street. The moving child is exciting, worth barking at. Once the motion is over, the dog calms down.

Objects that seem everyday and ordinary to you might be complicated for a dog. What could be simpler than, say, your own hand? But your dog experiences a hand petting his head (nice) as a different thing from a hand pressing down on his head (many dogs find this disturbing). The way the hand moves is part of what it is to the dog, and part of whether it's pleasant (petting) or worrying (pressing).

Watch a dog and you will see how he interacts with the world. Does a dog stare at a blank spot on the wall? Perk up his ears at "nothing"? Become fascinated by something in the bushes that you can't see? What your brain says is "nothing" the dog's brain says is "something." You and that dog may be walking side by side, but you are experiencing two different worlds.

ALEXANDRA HOROWITZ

A Dog's World Is Full of Details

As human beings grow from tiny infants to full adults, we have to learn how to manage our own senses. The world is awash in details of color, form, space, sound, texture, smell. If we noticed everything all the time, we couldn't get anything done. So we learn to tune things out. We narrow our focus. We choose what to pay attention to and let the rest fall away.

But those details still exist, and dogs notice them. A dog's senses can take in the details we don't let ourselves see. Dogs, of course, cannot see or hear or smell everything. But they do notice much of what we ignore.

Dogs cannot see as many colors as we can, but their eyes are more sensitive to contrasts between light and dark. If you've ever noticed a dog hesitate before stepping into a pool of water that is reflecting bright sunlight, or seem fearful about entering a dark room, you are seeing how their eyes react to bright lights and darkness. With eyes that are excellent at seeing motion, they notice things like a deflating balloon wafting near the curb. They don't quite understand words, but they hear the way our voices rise and fall, and they notice a yell or a silence.

Dogs also notice *new* things, just as we do. Our attention can be caught by a new smell or a startling sound. Dogs, who can smell and hear more than we can, are bombarded by new sensations, on the alert all the time. Things that we become used to—car doors slamming,

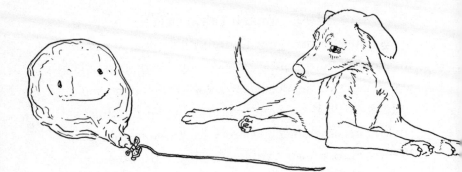

say—may be new *every single time* to a dog.

They notice things. We tap our fingers, we cough—and they look up. We shift in our seats—maybe we're getting up! We scootch forward in a chair—something must be happening! We scratch an itch, we shake our heads—these are fascinating movements, and they come with interesting smells, too, perhaps a whiff of perfume or shampoo. To all of this, dogs pay attention.

A Dog's World Is in the Moment

Dogs notice details. But they may not see the big picture. A dog knows the tree he is sniffing. He may not be aware of the forest all around him.

Dogs think. They make choices. They consider their options. But we don't have any evidence that dogs spend their time thinking about things that are not right in front of them. This is what it means to live *in the moment*, to be full of what you are seeing, smelling, tasting, thinking, feeling this very second.

ALEXANDRA HOROWITZ

A Dog's World Is Fleeting and Fast

We see the world; dogs smell it. And smelling is a different thing than seeing.

For a dog, smell tells time. Dogs know the past from smells that have weakened or faded or been covered by newer, fresher smells. They know the future from hints on the breeze. Seeing is something that happens mostly in the present. We see a blooming rose today; we cannot see the bud it was yesterday. Animals who live by their noses, like dogs, can smell a bit of the past and catch a glimpse of the future at the same time that they are smelling what exists right here, right now.

Smells have a lifetime. They move, they grow stronger, they fade away. For a dog, the world of smells is always in motion. It waves and shimmers in front of his nose.

And the dog must keep sniffing to stay aware of the world. As long as our eyes are open, we see without making much effort. But a dog's nose must keep working, and a dog must keep that nose moving. They race from spot to spot. They take in every smell. They are always on the alert to the way their world changes right in front of them.

A Dog's World Is Written All over His Face

Pump has a smile. It's one of the panting faces she puts on. Not every panting face is a smile, but every smile is a panting face. Her eyes can be wide open (excited, alert) or half

closed (contented). And her eyebrows and
eyelashes exclaim.

Dogs are honest. Their bodies do not deceive us. Your dog's joy when you come back home is obvious in his tail. His concern is right there in his eyebrows. Pump's smile is not an actual grin, but as she pulls back her lips to show a glimpse of teeth, she is letting me know how she feels. She's happy.

You can tell a lot about a dog by watching his head. It will tell you how he feels and what he's interested in. Think of a dog prancing around in front of others, tail and head high, with a stolen toy in his mouth. This is a clear gesture, something like pride. Young wolves will flaunt food in front of older animals in the same way.

What the head doesn't tell us, the tail does. High, low, wagging, or still, the tail is a signal of what's going on inside.

What is it like to be a dog? Keep watching your dog. He will tell you.

If everything I said about dogs in this book turned out to be wrong, I'd be surprised. But I'd be even more surprised if everything I said is right.

ALEXANDRA HOROWITZ

Trying to figure out what is happening "inside of a dog" means using imagination as well as information. There are things going on inside your dog, inside any dog, that we will probably never understand.

But we can try. We can always remember that dogs see the world in their own way. And if we look carefully enough, we may surprise our dogs with how much we get right.

10

YOU HAD ME AT HELLO

I walk in the door and Pump wakes up. First I
hear her: the *thump-thump* of her tail against
the floor, her toenails scratching on the ground
as she rises, the jingle of her collar tags as she
wriggles a shake down the length of her body
and out of her tail. Then I see her: Her ears
press back, her eyes soften. She smiles without
smiling. She trots to me, her head slightly down,
ears perked, tail swinging. As I reach forward
she snuffles a greeting. I snuffle back. Her damp
nose just touches me. Her whiskers sweep my
face. I'm home.

This is such an ordinary scene, dog and human,
together at the end of the day. It happens so many
times, in so many homes, that we don't stop to think very
much about it.

But we should. The deep connection between people
and dogs is actually very uncommon. It is not just any

animal who waits for your arrival. This particular animal, the dog, became what he is because humans domesticated dogs, took them into their homes. And then this particular dog, *your* dog, became part of your family.

Scientists call this the "dog-human bond."

ALL ANIMALS TOGETHER

Animals form bonds with each other. They mate. Some cooperate to raise young. Some live together for protection or companionship.

The most obvious bond among animals is something called the pair-bond, where two animals stay together after mating. They care for each other. They greet each other when they have been apart. Pairing for life can make it easier to produce young who will survive. A pair of animals can watch out for each other, share food, protect each other from predators. All of this can help a mate stay healthy and safe, which increases the chance of babies making it to adulthood.

Animals don't just bond in twos. Several animals can bond together in a herd or a pack, staying together because it helps them survive. Humans and dogs are both good examples of this kind of bonding. From the time of our long-ago ancestors, we have been social animals, living in groups. It was useful to do so. Dog ancestors and human ancestors bonded with others of their kind to hunt, to find mates, and to look after young. Like many other animals, we have bonding in our instincts.

But dogs and humans do something that is not so common. We create a bond with animals who are not of our own species. Dogs bond with people; people bond with dogs.

Why do we do this? Dogs and people are not forming a bond in order to raise babies or puppies, kill large prey, or defend a territory. And humans don't bond with other social animals—meerkats, say, or ants, or beavers. There must be more to it to explain why, out of all the social animals in the world, humans and dogs found each other.

Some of the reasons are simple. Dogs are easy to have around. Their natural rhythms of sleep and wakefulness match ours. They are ready to be awake when we are ready to take them out, asleep when we can't. They are a good size, some small enough to be picked up, some larger, but nothing that the average-size house can't handle. We can leave them by themselves for long stretches of time. They are trainable. They can keep us company for many years. Their bodies seem familiar—they aren't as bizarre to us as, say, a jellyfish or a star-nosed mole.

Finally, they're cute.

It is natural for humans to coo at puppies. We're attracted to certain features: large heads, short limbs, big eyes, teeny fingers and toes. These are what we notice most about human infants. Dogs have some of these features too. Their heads are big for their bodies; their eyes are large; their noses are either squashed or huge, never nose-sized. We can't help but find them cute.

So some of the reasons humans and dogs stay together come from our instincts. Our instincts tell us to bond with others and to take care of small, cuddly things with large eyes. And then this bond is maintained in three ways: through touch, through greeting, and through moving together.

Touching Animals

Neither of us is truly comfortable, but neither of us moves. He is on my lap, sprawled across my thighs, his legs dangling down the side of the chair. He's settled his chin on my right arm, right in the crook of my elbow. To type I have to pull my trapped arm up, my fingers just reaching the keyboard.

We named him Finnegan. We found him at a local shelter, in a cage among dozens of cages, all filled with dogs. I remember the moment I knew it would be Finnegan that we would take home. He leaned. Outside of his cage, on the tabletop where we were allowed to pet him, he wagged. His ears flopped around his tiny face. He coughed long bursts of coughs, and he leaned against my chest, his face tucked into my armpit. Well, that was that.

Often it is contact that draws us to animals. Petting zoos exist because people don't simply want to look at an animal on the other side of a fence—they want to touch. Better still if the animal is touching back, with a warm tongue or worn teeth grabbing at the food held out in your hands. Children and adults who come up to me on the street as I walk with my dog don't want to look at her, watch her wag, think about how she walks. No, they want to pet the dog. To touch her.

Dogs and humans share this longing. Children and parents touch and hug, and this contact isn't just pleasant. It's necessary. Without it, the child cannot develop normally.

Puppies love touch as well. Blind and deaf at birth, they huddle with their siblings and their mother. They cannot hear or see their family, but they can touch it, and they do. This begins a dog on a lifetime of relationships that are all about touching.

Wolves make a move to touch one another at least six times an hour. They lick. They nuzzle. They even touch when they are displeased with each other—pushing, pinning with a bite, or grabbing another wolf's muzzle or head in the mouth.

When a dog is with a human, this urge to touch means that they will burrow a head under our sleeping bodies or rest that head on us. They may push or bump us as we walk. They lick or gently nibble. In turn, they let us touch them. Dogs are extremely touchable, soft and furry, right there next to our dangling fingers.

How does it feel to a dog when we touch him?

First, keep in mind that touch is different on different parts of the body. You know this from your own body. Some areas are more sensitive than others. If somebody touches the back of your neck with two fingers a centimeter apart, you will feel two different touches. If those same two fingers are moved down the back, you will only feel a single touch. Your skin feels the touch differently in different places.

Dogs are the same, and at the same time not the same. They feel touch differently in different places, but their most tender areas are different from ours. Their whiskers, for example, are extremely sensitive to pressure and are important for sensing motion near the snout. This is one of the reasons why grabbing a dog's head or muzzle is an aggressive move. It is how a mother dog scolds a naughty puppy or what an older wolf may do to a younger one. A gentle tug on a tail is a different kind of touch. It will make a dog respond, but it is usually seen as play, not threat—unless you don't let go.

You can discover, just by seeing how your dog reacts to touch, what his most sensitive areas are. It matters not only *where* you touch, but *how*. Petting—when you touch the same area gently over and over—is different from pressure, when you hold a hand down on one area. Pressure is like shouting. It tells the dog the same thing petting does, but more strongly—sometimes too strongly. You might like it if a friend tells you something to your face, but not if she shouts it in your ear. Your dog may react the same way if you hold your hand down on his head and don't take it away.

Touching along the dog's entire body, however, can be something dogs love, especially when it was their idea. Dogs often find places to lie down that let them bring as much of their body into contact with yours as possible. Maybe this reminds them of their time as puppies, safely snuggled with their mother and brothers and sisters. It says they are safe and taken care of.

Saying Hello

Early in my life with Pumpernickel, I got a full-time job and she got a classic case of separation anxiety. In the mornings, as I prepared to leave the house, she began to whimper, follow me from room to room, and finally vomit. I talked to trainers who gave me advice about how to help her, and before too long Pump returned to her old self.

But there was one piece of advice that I did not follow. The trainers told me not to make a big deal of my return, not to celebrate our connection as I came home. I refused. Her snuffly

greetings, our reunion in a happy heap on the
floor, were too good to let go.

It's common to see animals greeting each other. If
one animal suddenly sees another in his den or territory, nervous excitement rises. The animal might attack
the newcomer. Or he might turn that excitement into a
greeting.

When mother and father wolves return to the den, the
pups mob them. The young wolves frantically lick at their
parents' faces, hoping this will make them vomit up some
half-digested food. The young ones take their parents'
muzzles in their mouths, nudge with their noses, take on
submissive postures, and wag furiously.

Your dog likely does some of the same things when you
arrive home. Ears that were pricked to hear your arrival
fall flat against the head, which dips slightly, a submissive
gesture. The dog pulls his lips back and drops his eyelids, a
smile. He wags madly. He wants to run around wildly, but
he also wants to stay close to you. So he stays near, but his
tail beats back and forth, full of the energy that his body
will not let out.

Your dog may even whine or yelp with pleasure to
see you. In the wild, wolves howl every day. Making
noise together is part of what keeps a pack close. If you
greet your dog with happy noise and "hellos," your dog
may make noise back at you. In all that he's doing, your

dog is showing that he knows who you are and is glad you've come home.

Dancing Together

Touching and greeting—is this all that bonds humans and dogs together? Not quite. Other animals are social as well. Other animals like to touch and greet each other. But there is one other thing that only humans and dogs share.

Timing. We act well together. We move to the same rhythm.

> On a long walk, Pump stays near me, but not too near. If she's ahead, she *checks*, looking back to see where I am. If I ever lag, she turns all the way around, ears up, waiting for me. Oh, how I love to approach her as she waits like this. If I skip into a gallop, she might play-bow, or swing around on her rear legs and trot off on our walk once more.

A house mouse, its heart beating four hundred times a minute, is always in a hurry. A tick can wait, motionless, for a month, a year, or eighteen years to find something to bite. A dog lives much more at our pace. We can respond to what dogs do; they can respond to us. They dance with us.

A puppy at first refuses to walk on a leash or pulls you

down the sidewalk. In very little time, though, puppies learn to walk at roughly the same speed as their owners. They *match* us. We match them in turn. This matching behavior is used by all sorts of social animals to strengthen the bonds between them.

Once we take them off the leash, the dance continues. Sometimes I get to take my dogs on what I think of as the perfect walk—a dog off-leash in an open area, running in great circles around me as we go. If things are going extra well, we encounter half a dozen other dogs, and we play.

> I start it. I inch to where she's lying, and I put my hand on her paw. She pulls it away—and puts her paw on my hand. I place my hand over her paw again. More quickly now, she mimics me. We trade slaps until I laugh, breaking the spell. She stretches forward over her paws to lick my face.

Dogs play with dogs; dogs play with people. What makes play fun? I tried to figure this out, studying my videotapes, watching dogs and humans playing together: wrestling, chasing, tossing, fetching balls and sticks and ropes. Was there one particular thing that all the good playtimes had in common?

What I found was simple, but important. In the best games of play, one player's actions are based on the other's.

This gives a rhythm to the play. A player reacts to something the other does—a person throws a ball, a dog dashes after it. A dog lunges, a second dog lunges back. A dog might run with a person or with another dog, matching pace, side by side. Players act because of what their play partner does.

When a dog plays with us, responding to what we do, we feel that we understand each other. We're on this walk *together*. We're playing *together*. Our timing matches; our rhythm is in sync. Pick up the leash of any dog in your neighborhood, and suddenly you are walking together, like old friends.

WHY BONDING MATTERS

Our bond with dogs is strengthened by contact, by greetings, and by the timing that lets us do things together. And that bond strengthens us as well.

Simply petting a dog can relax you, can actually slow your racing heart or make nervous sweating stop. Living with dogs keeps your levels of stress lower. It might even be true that living with a dog helps to keep you healthier. And the same is true for dogs. Human company lowers a dog's level of stress. Petting can calm a dog's racing heart.

The bond between human and dog is so close it can become a reflex. An experiment tested one reflex—what happens when humans yawn. A yawn can be contagious: If you watch a friend yawn widely, you may find yourself doing the same. So do dogs. They can catch our yawns. Among all other animals, only chimpanzees yawn when they see others doing it.

Try it. Spend a few minutes yawning at your dog. (Try not to glare, giggle, or give in when he'd obviously like you to being doing something else—petting him or feeding him, probably.) If your dog yawns back, you can see for yourself how deep the connection between human and dog can be.

The bond changes us. It turns us into people who can communicate with animals—with this animal, this dog. We watch our dogs, we notice them, and a huge part of what we see in them is how they see us.

Dogs watch us back. They see us, they smell us. Of course we love our dogs for themselves, but we also love how deeply they know us.

THE IMPORTANCE OF MORNINGS

Pump changed my own *umwelt*, the world that I live in. She changed what it was like to be me.

Walking through the world with my dog, I began to imagine what *her* world was like. I enjoyed a narrow, winding path in a shady forest partly because of how much Pump enjoyed it. She loved the cool of the dark shade, of course, but she also loved zooming along the path, stopping only for marvelous scents along the sides.

I now look at city blocks and think of their sniffing possibilities. Where I'll choose to sit in the park—which bench, what rock—is based on where a dog at my side would have the best view, and the best smells. Pump loved large open lawns and high grass or brush. I came to love large open lawns and high grass or brush, too, thinking about how much fun she would have there.

I smell the world more. I love to sit outside on a breezy day.

Mornings matter more to me now. All the time Pump was with me, mornings were important because, if I woke early enough, we could have a long, off-leash walk together. I still have trouble sleeping in.

It has been a year now since Pump and I shared our last morning. It is a tiny bit of comfort, knowing how much she changed me, because that means she is still with me, even now that she can no longer walk beside me.

My life with Pumpernickel and my other dogs, as well as what I have learned from studying dogs, brings me closer to understanding what it is like to be a dog. I know more of why dogs behave the way they do. Dog behavior comes from their wolflike ancestors, from domestication, from the ways their senses work, and from the ways they watch and know people. When you get used to noticing and thinking about dog behavior, it becomes a habit to look at things from a dog's point of view.

Along the way, here are some ideas to keep in mind.

GO FOR A "SMELL WALK"

Most of us would agree that we go for walks with dogs for our dog's sake. But so often we take a human walk, rather than a dog walk. We want to make good time, to keep going, to get quickly to the post office and back. People yank their dogs along, tugging at leashes to get noses out of smells, pulling them past other dogs.

Your dog doesn't care about making good time. Think about the walk that your dog wants. Pump and I had several kinds of walks. There were the smell walks, where we barely made progress, but Pump inhaled every smell she could find. There were Pump's-choice walks, where I let her choose which way we went at every corner. There were runs where she agreed to run with me while I agreed to stop now and then and go in circles around her as she

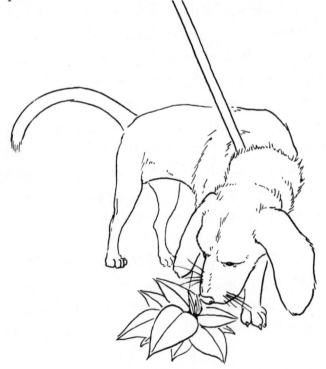

ALEXANDRA HOROWITZ

went in circles around an interesting dog. As she got older, there were even non-walking walks, where she lay down and just stayed put until she was ready to move on.

TRAIN THOUGHTFULLY

Teach your dog the things you want in a way he can understand. Be clear about what you want him to do. Be consistent; ask for the same thing in the same way every time. Tell him when he gets it right, with a quick reward. Good training comes from understanding the mind of a dog, knowing what he wants and how the world seems to him.

Remember, your dog is not born knowing what *come here* means. You have to teach him step by step, and reward him when he actually comes. Dogs pay attention to tiny clues from you. Make your clues clear.

Training can take a long time. Be patient. If you call to him to come and your dog doesn't come, don't chase him down and punish him. Your dog will connect the punishment with your arrival, not with the fact that you called, "Come!" five minutes ago. This is a good way to make him never come at all.

Once your dog has learned *come here*, there isn't that much more you have to teach him. Go on only if you and your dog enjoy it. What a dog mostly needs to know is the importance of you, and that's something dogs are born to see.

LET HIM BE A DOG

Allow for his dogness. Let him roll in *whatever-that-thing-is* once in a while. Let him splash through mud puddles. Walk off-leash when you can. When you cannot walk off-leash, do not yank him along by his neck, ever. Learn to tell a nip from a bite. Let two dogs who are getting to know each other smell each other's rumps.

CONSIDER THE SOURCE

Why does my dog do that? People ask me this all the time. Sometimes I just have to answer that there is no answer. When a dog suddenly flops on his back and looks at you, maybe he is just *lying down and looking at you*—nothing more. Not everything a dog does is full of meaning.

Of course, there are other behaviors that can be explained. You have to take into account what your dog is—an animal, a dog, a breed.

Breed matters. A dog who stares down invisible prey or stalks slowly toward other dogs is showing that he is a herder. A dog who is upset when one person leaves the room or who nips at your heels when you walk down the hallway is doing the same thing.

A dog who freezes when he sees movement in the bushes is pointing, showing you where prey might be. It may slow down your walk, but it's what a pointer is meant to do.

A dog who has been bred for work—but who doesn't have any work—may be restless, keyed up, have too much energy. Give him something to do. There is great science behind a simple game of fetch. A retriever is happy to bring a ball back to you again and again. It's part of what his breed is, part of who he is.

On the other hand, if your dog has a short nose and snuffles when he breathes, don't assume he can jog with you. He may not care for fetch, either. His eyes are not as good at catching motion as the retriever's are.

Animalness matters too. Don't treat your dog as a human. If you ask him to do something, make it something that comes naturally to an animal. We want our dogs to *heel*; some owners get furious if the dog doesn't. It might help to think about the fact that dogs (whose ancestors ran with a pack) are more likely to walk *near* their companion, not right on his heels. It's also true that most dogs have a preference for left or right, just as people are left- or right-handed. If you are always trying to make your dog *heel* to your left, you might both end up frustrated—especially if all the good smells are on the right side of the path. What matters most is that your dog is safe. Beyond that, let him walk like the animal he is.

And, finally, dog-ness matters. Your dog is a social creature. Company is important to him. You are important to him. Do not leave him alone for most of his life.

GIVE HIM SOMETHING TO DO

If you want to find out more about your dog, there is a simple way: Give him lots of choices. See what he likes.

Wiggle a string in front of your dog's nose along the ground. Stash a treat in a shoebox, or pick up an interesting dog toy from the pet store. Offer your dog a lot of different things to burrow into, nose, chew, bob, shake, chase, or watch. This will keep him occupied, and also keep him from trying to play with things you'd rather he left alone.

You can try agility training, where dogs are taught to climb, leap over, and get through objects on command. But you can also just offer your dog a winding path full of interesting smells or a field to explore.

Dogs like things that are familiar and things that are new. Happiness is new toys or new treats in a safe, well-known place. New things cure boredom. They occupy the dog's attention and offer something to do. Hiding foods to be searched for is another way to keep your dog from getting bored, since he must move around to find the treats, using nose and paws and mouth together.

PLAY WITH HIM

Dogs (especially when they are young) are always learning about their world, just like human children. Games that small children love work well with dogs, too. Peekaboo is good. Disappear under a blanket and watch your dog react, learning that you are still there even if you can't be seen.

Dogs are good at association, linking one event with another. You can play with that. Ring a bell before dinner, and dogs learn that the bell means dinner. You can connect bells or any kind of sound with food or other events—people arriving; time for a walk.

Play imitation games. If your dog does something, you do the same: Jump on the bed, yelp, paw the air.

Notice what your dog can already do, and try to help him do more. If he seems to know the words "walk" or "ball," start using more words: "smell walk," "squeaky ball." Then try "evening smell walk" or "blue squeaky ball." See how much your dog can learn.

Play with your dog as another dog would. Choose your play signal—slap hands on the ground, pant close to his face, race away and look back at him. And then play. Treat your hands as he does his mouth and grab head, legs, tail, belly.

(Give him a good toy to hold on to, or be prepared for some nips.) Maybe your own tail will begin to sway, just like his.

LOOK AGAIN

Just paying more attention to what your dog is doing can be a lot of fun. Notice the interesting and creative ways your dog tries to get your attention. Does he bark? Stare at you? Sigh loudly? Walk back and forth between you and the door? Lay his head on your lap? Pick the methods you like and respond to them, giving your dog the attention he wants. If you ignore the methods you don't like, he'll stop trying to use them.

Notice how your dog uses his eyes, how hard his nose works, how his ears fold back, prick up, and move toward a distant bark. Notice all the sounds he makes, and notice the sounds he notices.

Even the way your dog gets around can become interesting once you are paying close attention. A medium-size dog may use the classic *walk*. The right front and left rear paws will move together, but not perfectly in sync; the left front and right rear will do the same. If he's hurrying a little, he'll *trot*. The front-and-rear rhythm is close to perfect now, and he'll sometimes end up with three paws moving at once, only one touching the ground. Short-legged dogs like the bulldog tend to waddle a bit, the rear end waggling as they walk. Long-legged dogs do better at the *gallop* (watch a greyhound do this sometimes). The two back paws reach forward to hit the ground ahead of the front paws. Very small dogs *half-bound*, bringing their hind legs forward as a pair, but letting their front legs move one at a time. Other dogs *pace*, their two left legs moving forward and touching down, then their two right.

Which does your dog do?

SPY ON HIM

If you are wondering what your dog does at home all day when you are gone, videotape him. Whenever I got a glimpse of what Pump did when she didn't know I was watching, I saw her independence. She was freed from the need to check back in with me.

Most dogs are left alone all day, waiting it out until we return. Sometimes we're surprised and horrified when we come home to find that they have actually done something! If we thought more about their days, we wouldn't be so astonished. Dogs manage being left alone, but remember to give them something to do. Pay attention to what they need and want when you are around and when you're gone.

Each dog is different. Watching yours carefully (particularly when he doesn't know that you are watching) will tell you about yours.

DON'T GIVE YOUR
DOG A BATH EVERY DAY

Let your dog smell like a dog for as long as you can stand it. Some dogs will even develop painful skin sores from being bathed too often. And no dog wants to smell like a bathtub that has had a dog in it.

READ YOUR DOG

Dogs talk to us without words. Their faces, bodies, heads, and tails are all full of meaning. There's more to it than if the dog is wagging or barking, if you pay attention. A barking dog whose tail is wagging high is not about to attack—he is curious, alert, not sure about what's in front of him, and interested. A dog who snarls while guarding a favorite tennis ball, but whose tail is wagging low, is not

ALEXANDRA HOROWITZ

as fierce as he is acting—although he's definitely sending you a message about whose ball it is.

Remember that eye contact says a lot. You can get plenty of information about an unknown dog from his eyes, and from how he reacts to yours. Steady eye contact can be frightening for a dog. Don't come up to a dog you don't know without taking your eyes off him; he may think you are staring him down. If the dog is staring at you, you can turn your head a little, breaking eye contact. This tells the dog that you are not a threat. Dogs do the same thing, breaking a stare by turning their heads aside, yawning, maybe suddenly becoming interested in a smell on the ground.

If you think a dog is staring at you in a threatening way, look for more signs. Is the fur along his neck and back standing up? Is his tail up? Is his body frozen? If so, back away. But if a dog is staring at you while darting out a tongue to lick the air, the dog is telling you he adores you.

PET FRIENDLY

Not every dog likes to be petted. A dog who is sick, hurt, fearful, or who just doesn't want to be touched right now can respond with a snap if you don't pay attention to what he wants or likes.

For most dogs, the right touch by a human is calming and helps the dog feel connected to that person. Light touches tend to be irritating or exciting. Too heavy a touch feels overwhelming. Dogs can be calmed by steady strokes from the head to the rump. Watch your dog's reactions; he will tell you how he likes to be touched. And let him touch you back.

GET A MUTT

If you are planning on getting a dog, I have just the breed for you: the mutt. Some people will tell you that a mutt or a dog from the shelter is not as good as a purebred dog. This is simply wrong. Mutts are healthier, less anxious, and live longer than purebreds.

ALEXANDRA HOROWITZ

Particular breeds have been bred for particular jobs—herding, retrieving, hunting. If they are coming home to live with you as a pet, chances are they will not get to do that job. This can be hard for the dog and hard for the owner. Mutts, on the other hand, tend to be more easygoing. The hard edges seen in breeds are softened in a mutt; the drive inside them to retrieve things, herd things, or hunt things is less strong. They make comfortable companions.

KEEP YOUR DOG'S *UMWELT* IN MIND

On walks Pump was never satisfied with being on one side of the path or the other. She wove back and forth as I shifted the leash from my right hand to my left and back. Sometimes I'd insist that she stay on one side. She would sigh at me while we both glanced at the good unsmelled spots on the other side.

Even when we think of dogs in scientific terms, it's hard to resist using human words to describe them. We say that our dogs make friends, feel guilty, have fun, get jealous. We believe that our dogs understand what we mean, think about things, know better than to chew up our shoes. We can't help but think that they are sad, happy, scared, that they want, love, hope.

It's easy to talk and think like this. It's even useful

sometimes. But if we are always thinking of our dogs in human terms, we may lose sight of the animal in them. Maybe it just seems fun to shampoo our dogs, dress them up, and feed them doggy birthday cakes. But this is all part of making dogs seem less like animals and more like people.

If we really do forget that dogs are animals, we're in for some unhappy surprises. Dogs do not always behave just as we think they should. They may sit, lie down, roll over—but suddenly they will squat and pee in the house, bite your hand, jump on a stranger, eat something awful in the grass, ignore you when you call them, tackle a smaller dog. If we get frustrated when these things happen, it's because we forgot to remember that our dogs are animals. Our dogs are dogs.

You don't have to look at your dog the way a scientist would look at an animal she is running a test on. Scientists don't name their research subjects, for example. Of course you want to name your dog, love your dog, believe that your dog loves you. What would be the point of living with a dog otherwise?

But at the same time, remember your dog's *umwelt*, his "self-world." Think of how the world looks and smells and feels to him. Remember what matters to him and what he doesn't care about. Imagine, as far as you can, what is going on outside and inside his mind.

Go look at your dog. Go to him! Imagine his *umwelt*. And let him change your own.

ALEXANDRA HOROWITZ

POSTSCRIPT:
ME AND MY DOG

Pumpernickel wagged into my life in August 1990. We spent nearly every day together, until the day of her last breath in November 2006.

Pump was a total surprise. I didn't expect to be changed so completely by a dog. But I was drawn in by her. Before long, I felt pleasure in her company, pride at simply watching her do what she did. She was spirited, patient, willful, all in one great big furry bundle. She was sure of her opinions (she did not want to deal with yipping dogs), and yet open to new things (like friendships with the cats who now and then came to visit. No cat, however, was open to friendship with her).

Pump was never a subject for my research. Still, I brought her along with me when I went to watch dogs. She wanders through my videos of dogs at play. Now I wish I had sometimes turned the camera on her. Though I discovered much about dogs in general, I missed some of the moments of *my* dog.

Every dog owner would agree with me: Our dogs are special. All of them. But how can that be? If every dog is special, isn't special just—ordinary?

Not exactly. What is special about each dog is the way

his life joins with the life of an owner. What is special is the life story that dog and owner create together.

When Pump was nearly at the end of her life, you only had to look at her to see that she was old. She lost weight. Her muzzle grew gray. Sometimes, on walks, she slowed down or even stopped. I saw how many years had gone by for her, but when I looked into her eyes, she was a puppy again. I saw that tiny dog with no name who let us plop a too-big collar around her neck and walk her out of the shelter and the thirty blocks home. And then thousands of miles since.

Looking at Pump, I saw all of our life together.

After knowing Pump, and losing Pump, I met Finnegan. Already I cannot imagine not knowing him—this leaner on legs, this stealer of balls, this warmer of laps. He is not a bit like Pumpernickel. But all that Pump has taught me makes every moment with Finnegan richer by far.

She lifted her head and turned toward me. Her nose was dark and wet, her eyes calm. She began licking, full long licks of her front legs, of the floor. The tags of her collar clonked on the wood. Her ears lay flat, curling up a little at the bottom. She yawned. It was a long, lazy afternoon yawn. She settled her head down between her legs, breathed out a kind of *har-ummmp*, and closed her eyes.

ALEXANDRA HOROWITZ

Glossary

anecdote: a story, usually about a single, remarkable event. Scientists use the word "anecdote" to describe a story of a behavior that may be interesting, but that cannot be used as proof that that behavior is common or meaningful.

anal glands or sacs: small organs near a dog's anus (the opening for bodily waste) which may release an oily, foul-smelling liquid when the dog has a bowel movement or is frightened

ancestry: all of a living being's ancestors or family who came before him or her, including one's mother and father, grandparents, great-grandparents, and so on

assistant dog (also called service or guide dog): a dog specially trained to assist a disabled person. An assistant dog might help a blind person find his or her way safely or alert a deaf person to important sounds such as a doorbell, a telephone, or a crying baby.

attachment: a connection between two separate things, animals, or people

attention: noticing something in the environment, singling that thing out, and bringing it to the forefront of the mind. Attention means *considering* and thinking about what you are looking at or listening to.

attention-getter: an action meant to bring someone's attention to you. Dogs may use barking, touching, or getting close to you as attention-getters.

bond: a strong, meaningful, long-lasting attachment between two animals or a human and nonhuman animal

breed: a particular type of dog, such as a Labrador retriever or toy poodle. Members of a breed look similar and may have similar temperaments. A *purebred* dog is one whose mother and father were both members of the same breed. (See *purebred* and *temperament*.)

cancer: a serious disease that causes abnormal cells in the body to multiply in an uncontrolled manner

carbon copy: an exact or identical version

cognitive: about the brain, thinking, or sensing and understanding

communication: an exchange of information. Animals

and people have many ways of communicating, including words, sounds, touch, actions, and appearance.

contagious: tending to spread from one animal to another

Darwin, Charles (1809–1882): a British naturalist (a scientist who studies the natural world). Darwin was one of the first to propose the theory of *evolution*, or how species change in response to their environments, and how a species of animal can slowly, over many generations, change into a new species.

decibel: a unit of measurement for noise. A whisper is about fifteen to thirty decibels; normal conversation is about sixty. Nearby thunder is about one hundred twenty decibels.

domesticated: adapted (changed) to be well suited for life with human beings **domestication**: the process, which happens over many generations, of changing a wild animal into a tame one that can live with humans

dominant: said of a relationship between two animals: the one that is more assertive, instead of being more submissive

experiment: a scientific test of a hypothesis or idea

gaze: looking carefully at something. A gaze is directed attention to a part of the world.

gene: the coded instructions inside a cell for creating a certain form of life. Any living creature, from a blade of grass to a human being, has a set of genes inside each cell that provide instructions for building or maintaining that particular creature.

herder, herding dog: a member of a breed of dogs meant to monitor and limit the movements of other animals. Herding breeds include sheepdogs, collies, and German shepherds.

hertz: a unit of measurement for pitch, or how high or low a sound is. A low sound (such as an elephant's trumpet) is a few hertz; a high sound (such as a mouse squeak) is a large number of hertz.

imitation: a choice to do the same behavior as someone else in order to get the same result

instinctive: used to describe behavior that does not need to be taught; a reflex

IQ test: a test which is thought to measure intelligence. "I.Q." stands for "intelligence quotient"

iris: the colored ring around the pupil of the eye: It is a muscle that makes the *pupil* (the black part) larger or smaller in dark or light.

mirror test: a type of experiment designed to see if a human or nonhuman animal recognizes an image in a mirror as him or herself

obedience: following orders or directions given by another: With dogs, "obedience training" asks them to follow directions such as "sit," "stay," and "come."

pack: a group of animals that not only live together, they also cooperate in activities such as finding food or defending young and rely on one another for survival

pheromone: a chemical given off by a living creature, which usually causes another animal of the same species to behave in a certain way. Among other things, pheromones may announce when an animal is ready to mate, whether or not it is angry or aggressive, and whether it senses danger nearby.

pitch: how high or low a sound is

play signal: an action to communicate that one animal would like to play, or is about to play, with another

posture: the position of the body, especially upright or down

predator: an animal who hunts and eats others; a meat-eater

pupil: the dark circle in the center of the eye; its size is controlled by the *iris*.

purebred: an animal whose mother and father were of the same breed. See *breed*.

receptor: an organ or cell in an animal's body that can respond to sensory signals, like light, smell, or sound

retriever: a member of a breed meant to find and bring back prey for human hunters

rough-and-tumble play: play that involves wrestling, biting, and other moves that could be seen as aggressive if done outside of play

scavenger: an animal who eats prey that has already been killed or garbage left out by humans

subject: an human or nonhuman animal who is part of a scientific *experiment*

submissive: said of a relationship between two animals: the one that is less assertive

tame: (said of animals) not wild; comfortable interacting with humans

temperament: an inherited tendency to act or react in certain ways: personality

territorial: living in a particular location and actively defending that location from others

theory of mind: the ability to understand that another person or nonhuman animal's mind might be different from your own. Someone with a theory of mind knows, for example, that another person or animal might have beliefs, thoughts, and desires that may be different than their own.

tracking dog: a dog that has been trained to follow a scent trail. Tracking dogs are used, for instance, to locate lost people, rescue victims of natural disasters, and to find escaped criminals.

trainer: someone who teaches a dog to respond to certain signals with certain behaviors—often *obedience* commands

trait: a characteristic or feature. A trait might be physical, such as the size of an animal or the color of its fur. It may also be something about the way an animal behaves, such as a tendency to chase balls or track down prey.

umwelt (pronounced OOM-velt): the unique way a particular animal (including human beings) perceives and acts upon its surroundings: one's "self-world"

urine marking: releasing a small amount of urine from the bladder on purpose, in order to communicate with others

vomeronasal organ: an specialized body part, above the roof of an animal's mouth, which receives chemicals emitted by other animals and sends information about them to the brain

working dog: a member of a breed meant to perform a particular job. Retrievers, herders, and guard dogs are working breeds.

Notes and Sources

If you'd like to follow the research from our lab in New York City, go to this website: http://dogcognition.com.

The power of the dog's nose is illustrated in this Ted_Ed lesson: http://ed.ted.com/lessons/how-do-dogs-see-with-their-noses-alexandra-horowitz

CHAPTER 1:
FROM THE DOG'S POINT OF NOSE
on the dolphin smile:

Bearzi, M., and C. B. Stanford. 2008. *Beautiful minds: The parallel lives of great apes and dolphins.* Cambridge, MA: Harvard University Press.

on the fear grin in chimpanzees:

Chadwick-Jones, J. 2000. *Developing a social psychology of monkeys and apes.* East Sussex, UK: Psychology Press.

on eyebrow-raising in monkeys:

Kyes, R. C., and D. K. Candland. 1987. Baboon *(Papio hamadryas)* visual preferences for regions of the face. *Journal of Comparative Psychology,* 4, 345–348.

de Waal, F. B. M., M. Dindo, C. A. Freeman, and M. J. Hall. 2005. The monkey in the mirror: Hardly a stranger. *Proceedings of the National Academy of Sciences,* 102, 11140–11147.

on muzzle biting and standing-over in wolves:
Fox, M. W. 1971. *Behaviour of wolves, dogs and related canids.* New York: Harper & Row.

on umwelt and ticks:
von Uexküll, J. 1957/1934. A stroll through the worlds of animals and men. In C. H. Schiller, ed. *Instinctive behavior: The development of a modern concept* (pp. 5–80). New York: International Universities Press.

on dog kisses:
Fox, 1971.

on the dog's sense of taste:
Lindemann, B. 1996. Taste reception. *Physiological Reviews,* 76, 719–766.

Serpell, J., ed. 1995. *The domestic dog: Its evolution, behaviour and interactions with people.* Cambridge: Cambridge University Press.

"dogs have . . . a striking way of exhibiting their affection . . ."
Darwin, C. 1872/1965. *The expression of the emotions in man and animals.* Chicago: University of Chicago Press, p. 118.

CHAPTER 2:
BELONGING TO THE HOUSE

on the meaning of the word "domesticated":
I found this definition in Samuel Johnson's 1755 dictionary. *Domestical* and *domestick* are both defined, in part, as "belonging to the house; not relating to things publick."

on the variety of doglike animals:
Macdonald, D. W., and C. Sillero-Zubiri. 2004. *The biology and conservation of wild canids.* Oxford: Oxford University Press.

on the fox domestication experiments:

Belyaev, D. K. 1979. Destabilizing selection as a factor in domestication. *Journal of Heredity*, 70, 301–308.

Trut, L. N. 1999. Early canid domestication: The farm-fox experiment. *American Scientist*, 87, 160–169.

on wolf behavior and anatomy:

Mech, D. L., and L. Boitani. 2003. *Wolves: Behavior, ecology, and conservation.* Chicago: University of Chicago Press.

on domestication:

There are many theories on how dogs became domestic animals. The one in this book is supported by both the most recent research into dogs and their genes. It is set out in R. Coppinger and L. Coppinger. 2001. *Dogs: A startling new understanding of canine origin, behavior, and evolution.* New York: Scribner.

Clutton-Brock, J. 1999. *A natural history of domesticated mammals*, 2nd ed. Cambridge: Cambridge University Press.

on earliest date of domestication:

Ostrander, E. A., U. Giger, and K. Lindblad-Toh, eds. 2006. *The dog and its genome.* Cold Spring Harbor, NY: Cold Spring Harbor Laboratory Press.

Vilà, C., P. Savolainen, J. E. Maldonado, I. R. Amorim, J. E. Rice, R. L. Honeycutt, K. A. Crandall, J. Lundeberg, and R. K. Wayne. 1997. Multiple and ancient origins of the domestic dog. *Science*, 276, 1687–1689.

on development:

Mech and Boitani, 2003.

Scott, J. P., and J. L. Fuller. 1965. *Genetics and the social behaviour of the dog.* Chicago: University of Chicago Press.

on wolf rope task:

Miklósi, Á., E. Kubinyi, J. Topál, M. Gácsi, Zs. Virányi, and V. Csányi. 2003. A simple reason for a big difference: Wolves do not look back at humans, but dogs do. *Current Biology,* 13, 763–766.

on eye contact:

Fox, 1971.

Serpell, J. 1996. *In the company of animals: A study of human-animal relationships.* Cambridge: Cambridge University Press.

on breeds:

Garber, M. 1996. *Dog love.* New York: Simon & Schuster. Ostrander et al., 2006.

on breed specs:

Crowley, J., and B. Adelman, eds. 1998. *The complete dog book,* 19th edition. Publication of the American Kennel Club. New York: Howell Book House.

on sheepdog behavior:

Coppinger and Coppinger, 2001.

on packs:

Mech, L. D. 1999. Alpha status, dominance, and division of labor in wolf packs. *Canadian Journal of Zoology,* 77, 1196–1203.

Mech and Boitani, 2003, especially L. D. Mech, and L. Boitani. "Wolf social ecology" (pp. 1–34) and J. M. Packard. "Wolf behavior: Reproductive, social, and intelligent" (pp. 35–65).

on stray or free-ranging dogs:

Beck, A. M. 2002. *The ecology of stray dogs: A study of free-ranging urban animals.* West Lafayette, IN: NotaBell Books.

CHAPTER 3:
SNIFF
on sniffing:

Settles, G. S., D. A. Kester, and L. J. Dodson-Dreibelbis. 2003. The external aerodynamics of canine olfaction. In F. G. Barth, J. A. C. Humphrey, and T. W. Secomb, eds. *Sensors and sensing in biology and engineering* (pp. 323–355). New York: SpringerWein.

on the way a dog's nose works:

Harrington, F. H., and C. S. Asa. 2003. Wolf communication. In D. Mech, and L. Boitani, eds. *Wolves: Behavior, ecology and conservation* (pp. 66–103). Chicago: University of Chicago Press.

Lindsay, S. R. 2000, 2001, 2005. *Handbook of applied dog behavior and training* (3 volumes). Ames, Iowa: Blackwell Publishing.

Serpell, 1995.

Wright, R. H. 1982. The sense of smell. Boca Raton, FL: CRC Press.

on the vomeronasal organ:

Adams, D. R., and M. D. Wiekamp. 1984. The canine vomeronasal organ. *Journal of Anatomy*, 138, 771–787.

Sommerville, B. A., and D. M. Broom. 1998. Olfactory awareness. *Applied Animal Behavior Science*, 57, 269–286.

Watson, L. 2000. *Jacobson's organ and the remarkable nature of smell*. New York: W. W. Norton & Company.

on moist noses:

Mason, R. T., M. P. LeMaster, and D. Muller-Schwarze. 2005.

Chemical signals in vertebrates, Volume 10. New York: Springer.

on smelling us:
Lindsay, 2000.

on distinguishing twins by scent:
Hepper, P. G. 1988. The discrimination of human odor by the dog. *Perception*, 17, 549–554.

on bloodhounds:
Lindsay, 2000.

Sommerville and Broom, 1998.

Watson, 2000.

on using footsteps to detect a trail:
Hepper, P. G, and D. L. Wells. 2005. How many footsteps do dogs need to determine the direction of an odour trail? *Chemical Senses*, 30, 291–298.

Syrotuck, W. G. 1972. *Scent and the scenting dog.* Mechanicsburg, PA: Barkleigh Productions.

on the smell of tuberculosis:
Wright, R. H. 1982. *The sense of smell.* Boca Raton, FL: CRC Press.

on the smell of disease:

Drobnick, J., ed. 2006. *The smell culture reader.* New York: Berg.

Syrotuck, 1972.

on cancer detection:
McCulloch, M., T. Jezierski, M. Broffman, A. Hubbard, K. Turner, and T. Janecki. 2006. Diagnostic accuracy of canine

scent detection in early and late-stage lung and breast cancers. *Integrative Cancer Therapies*, 5, 30–39.

Williams, H., and A. Pembroke. 1989. Sniffer dogs in the melanoma clinic? *Lancet*, 1, 734.

Willis, C. M., S. M. Church, C. M. Guest, W. A. Cook, N. McCarthy, A. J. Bransbury, M. R. T. Church, and J. C. T. Church. 2004. Olfactory detection of bladder cancer by dogs: Proof of principle study. *British Medical Journal*, 329, 712–716.

on anal sacs:
Harrington and Asa, 2003.

Natynczuk, S., J. W. S. Bradshaw, and D. W. Macdonald. 1989. Chemical constituents of the anal sacs of domestic dogs. *Biochemical Systematics and Ecology*, 17, 83–87.

on anal sacs and vets:
McGreevy, P. (personal communication).

on scratching the ground after marking:
Bekoff, M. 1979. Ground scratching by male domestic dogs: A composite signal. *Journal of Mammalogy*, 60, 847–848.

CHAPTER 4:
DOG TALK
on the dog's hearing range:
Harrington and Asa, 2003.

on alarm clocks:
Bodanis, D. 1986. *The secret house: 24 hours in the strange and unexpected world in which we spend our nights and days.* New York: Simon & Schuster.

on dogs' response to high-pitched sounds:
McConnell, P. B. 1990. Acoustic structure and receiver response in domestic dogs, *Canis familiaris. Animal Behaviour*, 39, 897–904.

on Rico and other dogs who seem to understand words:
Kaminski, J. 2008. Dogs' understanding of human forms of communication. Paper presented at the Canine Science Forum, Budapest, Hungary.

Kaminski, J., J. Call, and J. Fischer. 2004. Word learning in a domestic dog: Evidence for "fast mapping." *Science*, 304, 1682–1683.

Pilley, J. W., Allison K. Reid. 2011. Border collie comprehends object names as verbal referents. *Behavioural Processes*, 86, 184–195.

on whimpers, barks, and other sounds dogs make:
Bradshaw, J. W. S., and H. M. R. Nott. 1995. Social and communication behaviour of companion dogs. In J. Serpell, ed., *The domestic dog: Its evolution, behaviour, and interactions with people* (pp. 115–130). Cambridge: Cambridge University Press.

Cohen, J. A., and M. W. Fox. 1976. Vocalizations in wild canids and possible effects of domestication. *Behavioural Processes*, 1, 77–92.

Harrington and Asa, 2003.

Tembrock, G. 1976. Canid vocalizations. *Behavioural Processes*, 1, 57–75.

on growls:
Faragó, T., F. Range, Zs. Virányi, and P. Pongrácz. 2008. The bone is mine! Context-specific vocalization in dogs. Paper presented at Canine Science Forum, Budapest, Hungary.

on laughs:
Simonet, O., M. Murphy, and A. Lance. 2001. Laughing dog: Vocalizations of domestic dogs during play encounters. Animal Behavior Society conference, Corvallis, OR.

on dog and wolf sounds:
Fox, 1971.

Harrington and Asa, 2003.

on kinds of barks:
Molnár, C., P. Pongrácz, A. Dóka, and Á. Miklósi. 2006. Can humans discriminate between dogs on the base of the acoustic parameters of barks? *Behavioural Processes*, 73, 76–83.

Yin, S., and B. McCowan. 2004. Barking in domestic dogs: Context specificity and individual identification. *Animal Behaviour*, 68, 343–355.

on hackles:
Harrington and Asa, 2003.

on tails:
Bradshaw and Nott, 1995.

Harrington and Asa, 2003.

Schenkel, R. 1947. Expression studies of wolves. *Behaviour*, 1, 81–129.

on posture:
Fox, 1971.

Goodwin, D., J. W. S. Bradshaw, and S. M. Wickens. 1997. Paedomorphosis affects agonistic visual signals of domestic dogs. *Animal Behaviour*, 53, 297–304.

on intentional communication:
Kaminski, J. 2008.

on bladders' single use:
Sapolsky, R. M. 2004. Why zebras don't get ulcers. New York: Henry Holt & Company.

on urine marking:
Lindsay, 2005.

Lorenz, K. 1954. Man meets dog. London: Methuen.

Bekoff, M. 1979. Scent-marking by free ranging domestic dogs. Olfactory and visual components. *Biology of Behaviour*, 4, 123–139. Bradshaw and Nott, 1995.

Pal, S. K. 2003. Urine marking by free-ranging dogs (Canis familiaris) in relation to sex, season, place and posture. *Applied Animal Behaviour Science*, 80, 45–59.

CHAPTER 5:
DOG-EYED

on the visual range of dogs and their relatives:
Harrington and Asa, 2003.

Miklósi, Á. 2007. *Dog behavior, evolution, and cognition.* Oxford: Oxford University Press.

on how a dog's eyes work:
McGreevy, P., T. D. Grassia, and A. M. Harmanb. 2004. A strong correlation exists between the distribution of retinal ganglion cells and nose length in the dog. *Brain, Behavior and Evolution*, 63, 13–22.

Neitz, J., T. Geist, and G. H. Jacobs. 1989. Color vision in the dog. *Visual Neuroscience*, 3, 119–25.

on Frisbee-catching:
Shaffer, D. M., S. M. Krauchunas, M. Eddy, and M. K. McBeath. 2004. How dogs navigate to catch frisbees. *Psychological Science*, 15, 437–441.

CHAPTER 6:
SEEN BY A DOG
on avoiding the gaze of a dominant animal:
Bradshaw and Nott, 1995.

on dogs looking at faces:
Miklósi et al., 2003.

on human babies and the way they look at the world:
The information about infants' visual abilities comes from a century of research. A nice summary is given in Smith, P. K., H. Cowie, and M. Blades. 2003. *Understanding children's development*. Malden, MA: Blackwell Publishing.

on following a pointing gesture:
Soproni, K., Á. Miklósi, J. Topál, and V. Csányi. 2002. Dogs' responsiveness to human pointing gestures. *Journal of Comparative Psychology*, 116, 27–34.

on gaze-following:
Agnetta, B., B. Hare, and M. Tomasello. 2000. Cues to food location that domestic dogs (Canis familiaris) of different ages do and do not use. *Animal Cognition*, 3, 107–112.

on attention-getting:
Horowitz, A. 2009. Attention to attention in domestic dog

(Canis familiaris) dyadic play. *Animal Cognition*, 12, 107–118.

on slurping to get attention:
Gaunet, F. 2008. How do guide dogs of blind owners and pet dogs of sighted owners (Canis familiaris) ask their owners for food? *Animal Cognition*, 11, 475–483.

on showing:
Hare, B., J. Call, and M. Tomasello. 1998. Communication of food location between human and dog (Canis familiaris). *Evolution of Communication*, 2, 137–159.

Miklósi, Á., R. Polgardi, J. Topál, and V. Csányi. 2000. Intentional behavior in dog-human communication: An experimental analysis of "showing" behaviour in the dog. *Animal Cognition*, 3, 159–166.

on retrieving games:
Gácsi, M., Á. Miklósi, O. Varga, J. Topál, and V. Csányi. 2004. Are readers of our face readers of our minds? Dogs (Canis familiaris) show situation-dependent recognition of human's attention. *Animal Cognition*, 7, 144–153.

on manipulating attention:
Call, J., J. Brauer, J. Kaminski, and M. Tomasello. 2003. Domestic dogs (Canis familiaris) are sensitive to the attentional state of humans. *Journal of Comparative Psychology*, 117, 257–263.

Schwab, C., and L. Huber. 2006. Obey or not obey? Dogs (Canis familiaris) behave differently in response to attentional states of their owners. *Journal of Comparative Psychology*, 120, 169–175.

on begging experiments:
Cooper, J. J., C. Ashton, S. Bishop, R. West, D. S. Mills, and R. J. Young. 2003. Clever hounds: Social cognition in the domestic

dog (Canis familiaris). *Applied Animal Behaviour Science*, 81, 229–244.

on attending to a video projection:
Pongrácz, P., Á. Miklósi, A. Doka, and V. Csányi. 2003. Successful application of video-projected human images for signalling to dogs. Ethology, 109, 809–821.

on why commands over a speaker don't work:
Virányi, Zs., J. Topál, M. Gácsi, Á. Miklósi, and V. Csányi. 2004. Dogs can recognize the behavioural cues of the attentional focus in humans. *Behavioural Processes*, 66, 161–172.

CHAPTER 7:
DOGS WHO STUDY HUMANS
on telling the difference between threatening and friendly strangers:
Vas, J., J. Topál, M. Gácsi, Á. Miklósi, and V. Csányi. 2005. A friend or an enemy? Dogs' reaction to an unfamiliar person showing behavioural cues of threat and friendliness at different times. *Applied Animal Behaviour Science*, 94, 99–115.

CHAPTER 8:
THE MIND OF A DOG
on understanding that unseen things exist:
Miklósi, 2007.

on string-pulling:
Osthaus, B., S. E. G. Lea, and A. M. Slater. 2005. Dogs (Canis lupus familiaris) fail to show understanding of means-end connections in a stringpulling task. *Animal Cognition*, 8, 37–47.

on how dogs notice and use human attention:
Erdohegyi, A., J. Topál, Zs. Virányi, and Á. Miklósi. 2007. Dog-logic: Inferential reasoning in a two-way choice task

and its restricted use. Animal Behavior, 74, 725–737.

on dogs looking to humans to solve task:
Miklósi et al., 2003.

on dogs following humans to get at food behind a fence:
Pongrácz, P., Á. Miklósi, K. Timar-Geng, and V. Csányi. 2004. Verbal attention getting as a key factor in social learning between dog (Canis familiaris) and human. *Journal of Comparative Psychology*, 118, 375–383.

on how human babies imitate:
Gergely, G., H. Bekkering, and I. Király. 2002. Rational imitation in preverbal infants. *Nature*, 415, 755.

on how dogs imitate:
Range, F., Zs. Virányi, and L. Huber. 2007. Selective imitation in domestic dogs. *Current Biology*, 17, 868–872.

on "do it" task:
Topál, J., R. W. Byrne, Á. Miklósi, and V. Csányi. 2006. Reproducing human actions and action sequences: "Do as I Do!" in a dog. *Animal Cognition*, 9, 355–367.

on theory of mind:
Premack, D., and G. Woodruff. 1978. Does a chimpanzee have a theory of mind? *Behavioral and Brain Sciences*, 1, 515–526.

on Philip, the dog who told where the key was hidden:
Topál, J., A. Erdőhegyi, R. Mányik, and Á. Miklósi. 2006. Mindreading in a dog: An adaptation of a primate "mental attribution" study. *International Journal of Psychology and Psychological Therapy*, 6, 365–379.

on the reasons why animals play:
Bekoff, M., and J. Byers, eds. 1998. *Animal play: Evolutionary,*

comparative, and ecological perspectives. Cambridge: Cambridge University Press.

Fagen, R. 1981. *Animal play behavior.* Oxford: Oxford University Press.

more on dogs' use of attention, attention-getters, and communication in play:
Horowitz, 2009.

on play signals:

Bekoff, M. 1972. The development of social interaction, play, and metacommunication in mammals: An ethological perspective. *Quarterly Review of Biology,* 47, 412–434.

Bekoff, M. 1995. Play signals as punctuation: The structure of social play in canids. *Behaviour,* 132, 419–429.

Horowitz, 2009.

CHAPTER 9:
INSIDE OF A DOG

on the "natural clock" inside the brain:
A nice review of some recent work: Herzog, E. D., and L. J. Muglia. 2006. You are when you eat. *Nature Neuroscience,* 9, 300–302.

Scientists have not spent much time studying boredom:
But there are a few studies. See Wemelsfelder, F. 2005. Animal Boredom: Understanding the tedium of confined lives. In F. D. McMillan, ed., *Mental health and well-being in animals* (pp. 79–91). Ames, Iowa: Blackwell Publishing.

on the mirror test:
Gallup, G. G. Jr. 1970. Chimpanzees: Self-recognition. *Science,* 167, 86–87.

Plotnik, J. M., F. B. M. de Waal, and D. Reiss. 2006. Self-recognition in an Asian elephant. *Proceedings of the National Academy of Science*, 103, 17053–17057.

Reiss, D., and L. Marino. 2001. Mirror self-recognition in the bottlenose dolphin: A case of cognitive convergence. *Proceedings of the National Academy of Science*, 98, 5937–3942.

on sheepdogs' knowing they are not sheep:
Coppinger and Coppinger, 2001.

on owners thinking dogs know right and wrong:
Pongrácz, P., Á. Miklósi, and V. Csányi. 2001. Owners' beliefs on the ability of their pet dogs to understand human verbal communication: A case of social understanding. *Cahiers de psychologie*, 20, 87–107.

on guilt experiments:
Horowitz, A. 2009. Disambiguating the "guilty look": Salient prompts to a familiar dog behaviour. *Behavioural Processes*, 81, 447–452.

Vollmer, P. J. 1977. Do mischievous dogs reveal their "guilt"? Veterinary Medicine, *Small Animal Clinician*, 72, 1002–1005.

on the blind Labrador Norman:
Goodall, J., and M. Bekoff. 2002. *The ten trusts: What we must do to care for the animals we love.* New York: HarperCollins.

on emergency experiment:
Macpherson, K., and W. A. Roberts. 2006. Do dogs (Canis familiaris) seek help in an emergency? *Journal of Comparative Psychology*, 120, 113–119.

on personal space:
Argyle, M., and J. Dean. 1965. Eye contact, distance and affiliation. *Sociometry*, 28, 289–304.

on the wolves' provocative showing of food:
Miklósi, 2007.

CHAPTER 10:
YOU HAD ME AT HELLO
on why we find infants and puppies cute:
Gould, S. J. 1979. Mickey Mouse meets Konrad Lorenz. *Natural History*, 88, 30–36.

Lorenz, K. 1950/1971. Ganzheit und Teil in der tierischen und menschlichen Gemeinschaft. Reprinted in R. Martin, ed., *Studies in animal and human behaviour, vol. 2* (pp. 115–195). Cambridge, MA: Harvard University Press.

on touch:
Lindsay, 2000.

on whiskers:
Lindsay, 2000.

on animals greeting each other after being apart:
Lorenz, K. 1966. *On aggression.* New York: Harcourt, Brace & World, Inc., p. 170.

on dog-human play:
Horowitz, A. C., and M. Bekoff. 2007. Naturalizing anthropomorphism: Behavioral prompts to our humanizing of animals. *Anthrozoös*, 20, 23–35.

on timing between dogs and people:
Kerepesi, A., G. K. Jonsson, Á. Miklósi, V. Csányi, and M.

S. Magnusson. 2005. Detection of temporal patterns in dog-human interaction. *Behavioural Processes*, 70, 69–79.

on dogs' effect on human health:
Friedmann, E. 1995. The role of pets in enhancing human well-being: Physiological effects. In I. Robinson, ed., *The Waltham book of human-animal interactions: Benefits and responsibilities of pet ownership* (pp. 35–59). Oxford: Pergamon.

Odendaal, J. S. J. 2000. Animal assisted therapy—magic or medicine? *Journal of Psychosomatic Research*, 49, 275–280.

Wilson, C. C. 1991. The pet as an anxiolytic intervention. *Journal of Nervous and Mental Disease*, 179, 482–489.

on other dog-owning benefits:
Serpell, 1996.

on contagious yawns:
Joly-Mascheroni, R. M., A. Senju, and A. J. Shepherd. 2008. Dogs catch human yawns. *Biology Letters*, 4, 446–448.

CHAPTER 11:
THE IMPORTANCE OF MORNINGS
on the way herding dogs behave:
Coppinger and Coppinger, 2001.

on handedness in dogs:
P. McGreevy. (personal communication).

on training:
For some ideas, see: McGreevy, P., and R. A. Boakes. 2007. *Carrots and sticks: Principles of animal training.* Cambridge: Cambridge University.

on preference for the new:

Kaulfuss, P., and D. S. Mills. 2008. Neophilia in domestic dogs (Canis familiaris) and its implication for studies of dog cognition. *Animal Cognition*, 11, 553–556.

on dog gaits:

Brown, C. M. 1986. *Dog locomotion and gait analysis*. Wheat Ridge, CO: Hoflin Publishing Ltd.

Acknowledgments

Thanks, first, to all the dogs. To Pumpernickel, who chose us at the shelter, for allowing me the incredible pleasure of knowing her for so many years. Thanks to the dogs of our family for teaching us: to Aster, Beckett, Chester, D'Arcy, Heidi. Thanks, ear tickles, and chest rubs to Finnegan and Upton, irrepressibly doggy, who give me ideas and give me great joy.

And so many people! One hears that books are difficult to write. If so, this is not a book, for it was a delight to write, as it is delightful to observe and be with dogs and think dog-thoughts full-time. I was lucky to find in graduate school people who would let me—and help me—study dogs: Jeff Elman, Shirley Strum, Mark Bekoff. Kris Dahl—and also Tina Wexler—at ICM; Colin Harrison, at Scribner; and now Kristin Ostby, have all made this book what it is. Thank you to Sarah Thomson, who adapted this book, for so keenly imaging What It Is Like to Be a Young Reader, stressing the content and jettisoning the inessential. It is a pleasure to work with you all.

I hatched the idea of *Inside of a Dog* with Damon Horowitz; he is owed great thanks for pushing me off that cliff. Everything ran by my parents, Elizabeth and Jay, and the success of this book is their success too. I am not the only writer in my house: Ammon Shea is a walking dictionary (but much more charming) and there is nothing I've written that isn't made better by his reading it.

And Ogden Thelonious Horowitz Shea: you are a whisker shy of being able to read this yourself. I can't wait until you can.

Index